LIFE'S WONDERS

I0683395

The Book Of Life

Michael Sandos

ARPress
ILLUMINATING IDEAS
EMPOWERING VOICES

ARPress
45 Dan Road Suite 5
Canton MA 02021

Hotline: 1(888) 821-0229
Fax: 1(508) 545-7580

Ordering Information:

Quantity sales. Special discounts are available on quantity purchases by corporations, associations, and others. For details, contact the publisher at the address above.

Printed in the United States of America.

ISBN-13:   Paperback   979-8-89389-772-2
               eBook   979-8-89389-773-9

Library of Congress Control Number: 2024922596

LIFE'S WONDERS

The

Book

Of

Life

Mind over Matter

Mind, Body, and Spirit

Life's Wonders

LIFE'S WONDERS

The Book of Life

Let Your Dreams come true.
Meet and Understand your brain.
Mind Power, Energy, Brain Waves,
The Body, Mind, and Spirit.
Right and Left side of the Brain.
Brain Waves, Vibrations, Rhythm
Mind's Conscious and Subconscious
Life's Energy! Rhyme, Vibrations
Activate Pineal Gland Brain Waves.
Have fun, enjoy The Book of Life.

It' amazing that
People carry their brain around
their whole life and never take
Time to meet their own Brains.
It's Easy, it's Fun, it's Amazing,
It's fast, It's powerful, take this
opportunity to finally meet your
Brain. Get every thing you want
and deserve. Attract Love, Money,
Knowledge, Energy, Success,
New Ideas, Let your Brain Wave
and the Universe Show you how!

Are Miracles Psychic Powers or are Psychic Powers Miracles

Use both Right and Let sides of the Brain discover true Mental
and Physical Power, Your Health, Wellness, Understand the
Creative Power of the Right side of the Brain in Collaboration
with the Physical Power of the Left side of the Brain

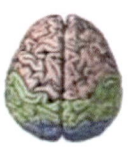
Life's Wonders
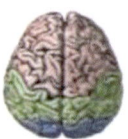

SENIORS OHAHA

Body, Mind & Spirit

Life's Wonders

BrainWaves
Vibration

SENIORS OHAHA
Body, Mind & Spirit

You need to exercise your brain at least **15 minutes** each day Just sit and think , meditate for 15 minutes on your growth. Create new vibrations for you to grow and develop yourself. Yes God gave you all the tools to get and do anything you want. You see your mind can not tell the difference between a memory or visuazation if you Imagined some thing. Example:

Rememb er a Island Island

Now

Imagine an Island

Just like this photo you can't tell the difference! Your mind is the same way it can not tell the difference of when you are imagining Something or if your simply remembering it. It's all the same to The Mind. Therefore you are what you believe yourself to be.

We use things like imagination and vibrations to build ourselves and mold ourselves into what ever we want to be. Does that make sense? It's easy think of some thing like music that really make your rhythm Come to surface it makes you smile and start moving with the sound Of the music. (did you notice there is no music there is just memory or imagination. Yet you were smiling and feeling the motion. Or should we say emotion! Point I you create vibration in your mind.

Life's Wonders

SENIORS OHAHA
Body, *Mind* *& Spirit*

The goals of are achieved through the development of relaxation, strength, endurance, flexibility, coordination, agility, mind-body communications; abiding by the laws of nature in respect to diet, body dynamics and mediation. Now think about it 3 things:

#1. How often do you breathe / all the time 24/7

#2. You now are simply reprogramming your Brain. The conscious mind is telling the Sub—conscious mind to relax and feel better with each breath that you take. From now on your mind will achieve relaxation within the effort. You have taking control of your body and mind.

For most folks it will take about 2 to 6 weeks to totally reprogram your brain and body to a daily natural state of body and mind function.

Also do these exercises every night when you go to bed and every morning just before you get up to start your day. Yes both to wake-up and to go to sleep. (Do this at least 7 times) each morning and evening.

Now you say why in the mornings this exercise will put oxygen Into your body, blood cells and giving you a better range of motion, flexibility and motion. You will get up and walk away feeling almost guilty about feeling so good.

Life's Wonders

SENIORS OHAHA

SENIORS OHAHA
Body, Mind & Spirit

Breathing

Take 7 breaths while saying to yourself

- **Inhale through your nose, Exhale through your mouth**
- If you breath through your nose your lungs fill.
- If you breath through Your mouth your tummy fills.

5 different chants or phrases that you will need to say to yourself each and every time you take a breath.

1. With each and every breath I take , I feel so **relaxed**, so much more relaxed than I have ever felt before.

2. With each and every breath I take , I feel so **good**, so much better than I have ever felt before.

3. With each and every breath I take , I feel so **recharged**, so much more recharged than I have ever felt before.

4. With each and every breath I take , I feel so **happy**, so much happier than I have ever felt before.

5. With each and every breath I take , I feel **stronger**, so much stronger than I have ever felt before.

Practice this every night in bed before you go to sleep! And every morning before you get up or as your getting up sitting on the bed. Remember 7 breathes **Inhale through your nose, Exhale through your mouth.** *After about 7 weeks of doing this you will notice you will fall asleep So much easier. In fact in the night if you awaken simply, **Take 7 breaths while saying to yourself** With each and every breath I take , I feel so **relaxed**, so much more relaxed than I have ever felt before and go to sleep.*

Life's Wonders

LIFE'S WONDERS

SENIORS OHAHA

SENIORS OHAHA
Body, Mind & Spirit

Life's Secrets

As you get more comfortable with this you will add 5 more chants or phrases of or requests of your own. As an example:

A. With each and every breath I take , I feel **a live**, so much a live than I have ever felt before.

B. With each and every breath I take , I feel **my immune system** working through my body healing, fixing all my injuries.

C. With each and every breath I take , I feel **more aware,** so much more aware than I have ever felt before. Add anything like
   I need money, or **I need to be more Knowledgeable**

D. **This one is very powerful, try to do this as much as possible! With each and every breath I take, I feel my Right Brain working with my left brain, and I feel smarter than I have felt ever before.**

You see your are simply attaching a very important function like Breathing to your sub-conscious mind to help you relax and get what ever you wish accomplished in life. Something like breathing because your sub-conscious makes sure you keep breathing to live.

Through controlled Motivation you now can achieve anything you wish to, simply by relaxing and programming your success.

Life is wonderful you body and mind are fantastic you are using your natural functions to succeed at anything you wish. It's very important that you read further in the book to understand why and how all these things work. You must understand them all in order to completely get the best results.

Life's Wonders

LIFE'S WONDERS

SENIORS OHAHA
Body, Mind & Spirit

Now as you can imagine you can use other chants to achieve even more fantastic controls in your life. As an example here are a few I use. Just rotate these chants in with your main relaxation chants.

• With each and every breath that I take, I feel more and more relaxed, I can feel my body healing any injury I may have throughout my body.

• With each and every breath that I take I feel more and more relaxed, I feel better and better than I have ever felt before.

• With each and every breath that I take I feel more and more relaxed, I can feel Happier and feel my left and right side of my brain working together (you see when you allow both sides of your brain to collaborate together you simply will be able to process more than ever before (some say that you will become a genius over night.)

With each and every breath that I take I feel more and more relaxed, I feel happier and feel more love in my life, more and better that ever before.

• With each and every breath that I take I feel more and more relaxed, I feel aware of everything around me.

You see these things are called Controlled Motivation you can control your life and every direction of it. Make your life more rewarding, enjoy every thing around you to the fullest. These are a few of the wonderful opportunities you have at your fingertips. You now have become "**aware**" aware of **self** aware of I the fact that you're in control smile to yourself, look at how powerful you are and how strong you will become simply by Breathing.

Life's Wonders

SENIORS OHAHA
Body, Mind & Spirit

Oxygen makes your body work, it feeds the body with Oxygenated blood, pushes the garbage to waste, operates the electrical system and make the repertory system function. Without oxygen to run the circulatory system things just don't work properly. How cool God made you. Fix yourself, heal yourself, become any thing you wish to be simply by breathing It's a very popular life style practiced around the world today. Ultimately, Breathing combined with Tai Chi Kung Fu is the mastery of a difficult task — the attainment of a standard of excellence, it could be described as a combination of many physical/mental disciplines including elements of dance, gymnastics, boxing, self-defense, weaponry, body-building, meditation, even running.

It's a holistic approach to health, fitness, healing, personal growth and self improvement. Kung Fu involves the development of the complete person. It is a way of life, a method of achieving and attaining the highest physical and mental development possible. Kung Fu builds strength and self-awareness, concentration, motivation, and directs and focuses one's mental and physical energies with coordinated synergy.

Life's Wonders

SENIORS OHAHA
Body, *Mind* & *Spirit*

Relax and put Your Mind to Sleep Quickly

If you often lay awake, unable to put your mind to rest while you're tossing and turning, you're going to love what you're about to read, because I'm about to share with you one of the most powerful methods for quickly shutting off your mind, and drifting off to sleep. As you may already know, your mind must be in the Alpha brain-wave stage to fall asleep. This is the stage your mind enters you're still conscious, but your body and begin to relax. It enables your more rampant and conscious mind to turn off as you enter the realm of sleep. We all know how it feels... when you're lying awake in bed trying to fall asleep, it seems like your mind is running on hyper-speed. It's almost like you're thinking 10 times faster than when you're just normally awake and alert. In fact, if you experience this often, I can tell you for a fact that your mind IS working harder than it is when you're not trying to fall asleep, and there is a very good reason for it, "Energy in motion, tends to STAY in motion" "Energy stopped, tends to STAY stopped" In other words, if you take action in your life, and begin to create success, you will experience more and more success every day. Success breeds success.

Life's Wonders

SENIORS OHAHA
Body, *Mind* *& Spirit*

The 3-Step Process for Controlling Your Mind
Step 1: Achieve Physical Relaxation 1st.
Awareness Redirect your mind and what you're thinking.
The first step Lay back and get as comfortable as you can.
Then feel yourself Breathing:
Inhale through your Nose, Exhale through your Mouth
Take one step at a time don't rush relax understand that
when you breathe through your mouth you fill your
tummy with air... And when you breathe through your
Nose you inflate your lungs, you want your lungs to inflate
all the looms or as much as possible. Understanding Multi-
tasking, the simple art of doing 2 or more things at a time.
Let's work on Multi- tasking your Mind, as you breathe simply
say to yourself the following chants.

With each and every breath that I take,
I feel more and more relaxed...
I feel better and better, I feel more and more relaxed than I
have ever felt before. Now you need to repeat this every time
you start to meditate. Later we will use this same technique
using many other Chants to get the things you want and need
in life love, health, knowledge, Money etc.

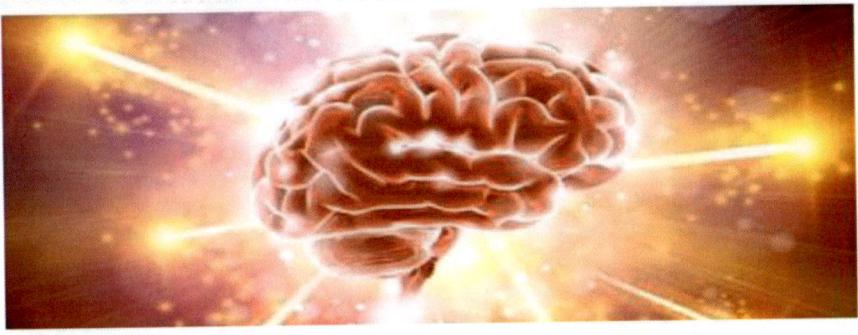

Life's Wonders

SENIORS OHAHA

"Breath of Life"

Seniors are the Kings and Queens of Our Time

Things to Know Only Kings, Queens and Gods were allowed to carry the Ankh symbol. The ankh is the Egyptian sign of life and indicates that the King or God holding it has the power to give life or take it away from lesser mortals. The Ankh as a symbol of the life giving elements of air and water. A God or Goddess would hold the Ankh before the King's nose, giving him the "breath of life" or as streams of water in the form of Ankhs running over the King during ritual purification. The Ankh was a scepter that was popular for Gods to hold it became a symbol of well-being and happiness for 5000 years..

Life's Wonders

LIFE'S WONDERS

Using Non-Conscious and Conscious Mind and Subconscious Mind

Mind over Matter Body, Mind, and Spirit

Brain Waves and Vibrations The Secrets of Life's Energy!

Exploring Time and Space It's your time and your Space

It's not hard to be who you are! It's believing in who you are!

Seniors Omaha The Secrets of a healthier more enjoyable life.

Seniors Ohaha *is an* **Ancient** *Chinese Art of Breathing and Living, combined with the Chinese Art of Tai Chi Kung-Fu exercise. It helps people regain flexibility, strength, range of motion, a better digestive systems, pleasant sleep awakening recharged, strengthen mind control and so much more. Have power over your life again. This is a journey of knowledge, experience and secrets of life for the young of all ages. It's mind over matter to take control of oneself. Turn negatives into positives by curbing your fear. This simple and easy process of learning to breathe correctly can strength your mental, spiritual and physical wellbeing by something that is so simple and yet so powerful.*

Life's Wonders

LIFE'S WONDERS

Using Left and Right side of the Brain
Left side of the Brain – Mechanical
Right side of the Brain – Creative

Understanding and use of the Brain Waves and Brain Vibrations

Alpha Brain Waves - Meditation, Relaxation

Bata Brain Waves – Energy, Mental, Spiritual

Delta Brain Waves – Healing, Sleep, Restorative

Gamma Brain Waves – Higher Brain Functions

Theta Brain Waves – Wealth, Success, Money
power to achieve Knowledge, Energy, Memory, anything you wish for.
Theta Waves the hidden key to Manifesting Abundance and Success.
Theta can help you Activate the Pineal Gland

Life's Wonders

Pineal Gland

How to activate your pineal gland.

Subconscious, Conscious Mind Use Theta Brain Waves, Vibrations, Rhyme, Sound Recordings, Visualization, Meditation, Manifesting. Activating your Pineal Gland tapping into levels of your higher-levels. The Pineal Gland is located between the left and right side of the Brain. Control your Physical and Metaphysical, Mind, Body and Spirit, getting everything you want and deserve in Life.

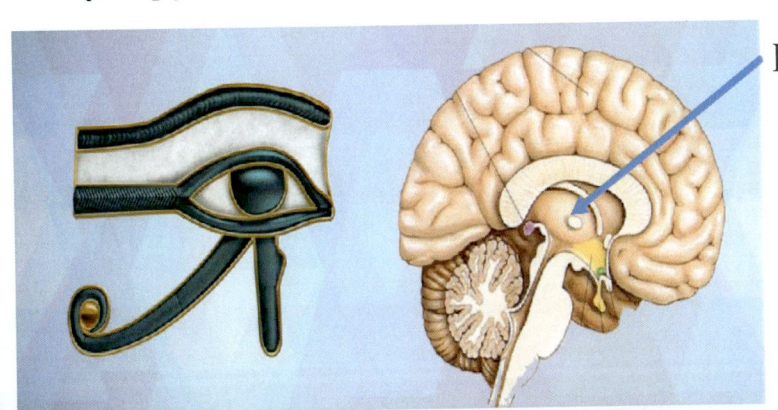

Pineal Gland

LIFE'S WONDERS

Unlocking the Pineal Gland requires a dedicated Meditation Practice. Here is a step by step guide.

1. Create a special space
2. Set your Intention
3. Relax and Breath
4. Deepen your awareness
5. Visualize and Activate
6. Seek Insight
7. Reflect and Record
8. Consistent Practice
9. Deepen Your Inner Connection
10. Expand Your Knowledge

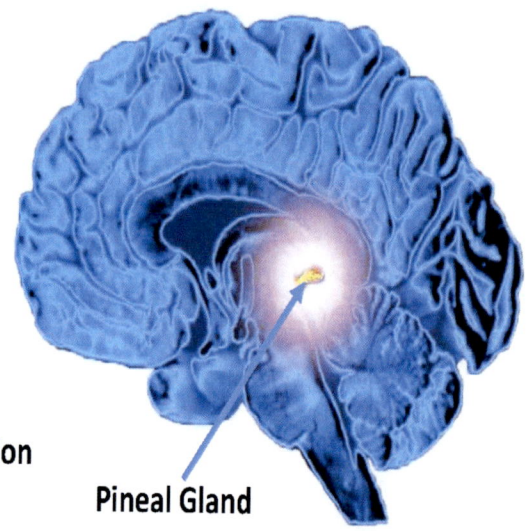

Pineal Gland

The concept of the Third EYE, Often associated with the Pineal Gland. Activating the pineal Gland through the THETA Brain Wave. And many other Manifestation concepts.

The Mystical Third Eye to Higher Consciousness

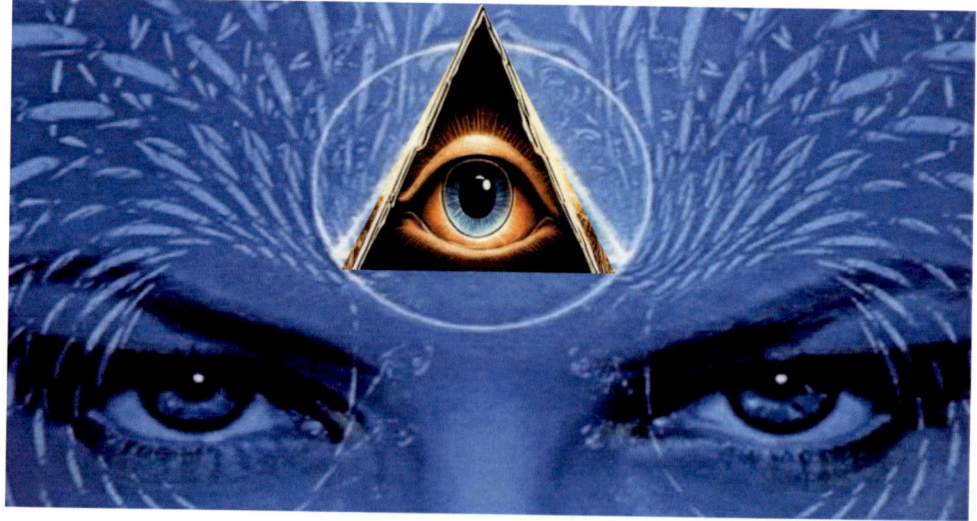

Life's Wonders

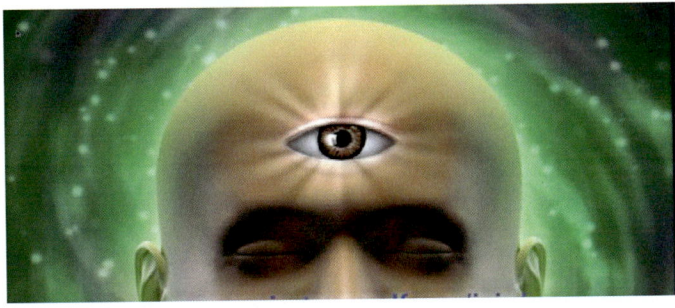

Activate your Minds Eye

Two Types of Meditation Passive and Active Meditation

All meditation systems, such as Yoga, Zen, Transcendental Meditation™, Silva Life System and others have similar benefits. By "passively" letting go and going within, we "deactivate" our survival mechanisms and allow our body's natural health and rejuvenation abilities to be activated. Each method has its own way of reaching the inner state of mind, and has it's own goals.

Active Meditation

These techniques allow you to use the relaxed, healthy state of mind that occurs during meditation to solve your day-to-day problems. We've found that by "actively" utilizing brain languages (kinesthetic, visual, and auditory thought processes), we can use this higher energy state to improve memory and learning skills, change unwanted habits, enhance health, and healing. He also developed techniques to achieve what many people call "tapping the super-conscious" to solve problems, reach goals, come up with new ideas and solutions to problems. Some students use the active system to enhance their spiritual growth. Using such techniques within a meditative state is called "active" meditation.

Your brain functions on a small amount of electricity, much like a computer. This electrical current vibrates and pulses at various speeds. When you are wide awake, with your eyes focused, your brain vibrates 20 times per second – what scientists call 20 cycles per second or the Beta frequency.

LIFE'S WONDERS

SENIORS OHAHA

Body, Mind & Spirit

Mind over Matter

What's on your Mind Does Matter

Life's Wonders

SENIORS OHAHA

Understand there are many different ways to
Get to Alpha, Beta Or to relax, release stress,
Achieving success in your life. Programs like
Jose Silva, Tapping, Quantum Jumping, Quantum physics,
Brain wave and more. I like Seniors Ohaha personally
because it helps build and rebuild my body functions all at
the same time! Because we are using the Natural path of
Oxygenation the body, the Repertory system the Human
electrical system our conscious & sub-conscious minds.
I believe that by using all or any of them together is
wonderful and you will just see that God has given us all
the tools to heal ourselves to gain health and success and
live our lives in happiness and joy Simply by breathing
correctly.

✓ The most important thing is to, **believe in yourself.**
✓ Next visualize yourself in the position and place you want.
✓ Next if you can't visualize than use your imagination.
✓ Exercise your brain 30 minutes daily, relax have fun.

Remember always: Action is an equal and opposite reaction
to make Opportunity and success yours.
THE POWER OF POSITIVE THINKING!

**Will power, persistence, new ideas, willingness, action and
courage, enthusiasm, faith, belief, use all your senses!
Remember**; *Understanding the brains state of Mind.*
**The Conscious mind uses 40 cycles per second to process
The Sub-Conscious mind uses 40 billion cycles per second**

**Allow your brain the opportunity to work and push it for
more exercise it as you would any muscle.**

Life's Wonders

SENIORS OHAHA

SENIORS OHAHA
Body, Mind & Spirit

YOUR Brain

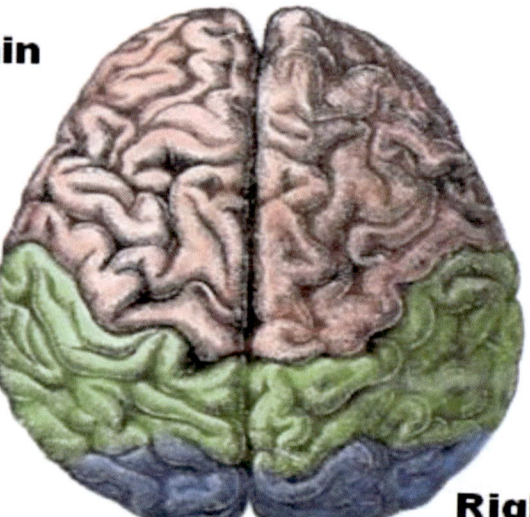

**Left Side
of your Brain**

**Right Side
of your Brain**

Most people use the **left side of the brain**, and most people **do not** use much of their brains.
Think about it, what if you could use **both sides** of the brain. Think, twice as much brain power, double your strength.

Become a **Genius** in seconds, have twice the power of your thinking and mental process, be able to problem solving faster and better than ever before. Be naturally smarter, quicker, faster, healthier all just because you use both sides of the brain. You need to spend 15 minutes per day thinking (**Learn to think**) You need to spend 15 minutes per day relaxing (**meditating**)

Life's Wonders

SENIORS OHAHA

Visualization, Imagination

Your mind can not tell if things are real or if they are made up! So anything you can think of, and or Imagine or visualize is real in your mind. Therefore the sky is the limit, using the right and left side of the brain will give you the power of the universe. Be a genius simply relax and use both sides of your brain.

Simply Breath

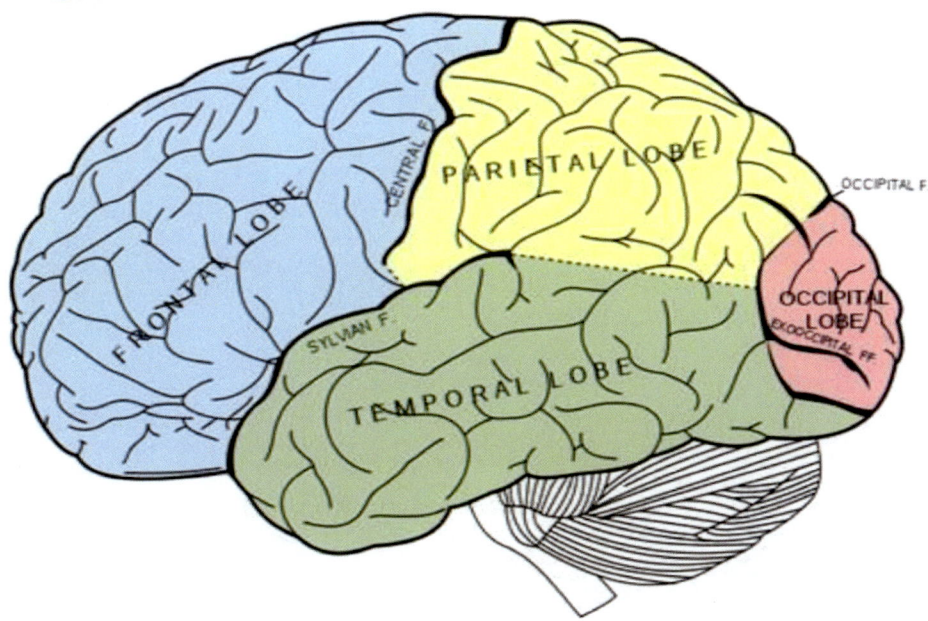

Keep it simple just talk to your Conscious mind and have it tell Your sub-conscious mind what you want it to do and it will reprogram your sub-conscious mind to do so.

Life's Wonders

RAS Reticular Activating System

Located at the bottom
of the nerve brain stem.

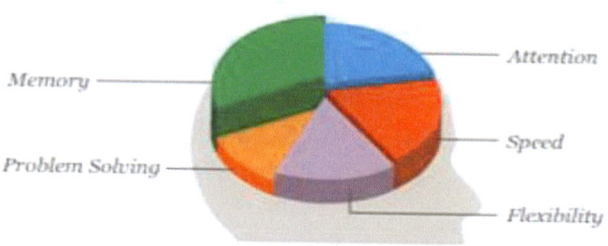

Memory — Attention

Problem Solving — Speed

Flexibility

What is this RAS? Imagine that you're walking through a busy noise airport passenger terminal. Think of all the noise - hundreds of people talking, music, announcements, luggage carriers.
How much of this noise is brought to your attention? Not a lot.
True, you can hear a general background noise, but not many of us bother to listen to each individual sound. But then a new announcement comes over the public address system - saying your name or maybe your flight. Suddenly **your attention** is full on. Your RAS is the automatic mechanism inside your brain that brings relevant information to your attention.

Your **reticular activating system** is like a filter between your conscious mind and your subconscious mind. It takes instructions from your conscious mind and passes them on to your subconscious. For example, the instruction might be, "listen out for anyone saying my name". There are some interesting points about your RAS that make it an essential tool for achieving goals.

Life's Wonders

LIFE'S WONDERS

SENIORS OHAHA

RAS   Reticular Activating System

First, you can deliberately **program** the reticular activating system by choosing the exact messages you send from your conscious mind. For example, you **set goals**, or say **affirmations**, or **visualize** your goals. Napoleon Hill said that we can achieve any realistic goal if we keep on thinking of that goal, and stop thinking any negative thoughts about it. Of course, if we keep thinking that we can't achieve a goal, our subconscious will help us NOT achieve it.

Second, your reticular activating system cannot distinguish between 'real events' and 'synthetic' reality. In other words it tends to believe whatever message you give it. Imagine that you're going to be giving a speech. You can practice giving that speech by visualizing it in your mind.

What we need to do is to create a very specific picture of our goal in our conscious mind. The RAS will then pass this on to our subconscious - which will then help us achieve the goal. It does this by bringing to our attention all the relevant information which otherwise might have remained as 'background noise'.

The reason psycho cybernetics is so important is that the RAS will prevent our goals messages getting through to our subconscious if our self-image is not congruent with our goals.

Did You Know That Meditating Just 15 Min a Day Could Change Your Life...

Life's Wonders

SENIORS OHAHA

RAS   Reticular Activating System

First, you can deliberately **program** the reticular activating system by choosing the exact messages you send from your conscious mind. For example, you **set goals**, or say **affirmations**, or **visualize** your goals.

Napoleon Hill said that we can achieve any realistic goal if we keep on thinking of that goal, and stop thinking any negative thoughts about it. Of course, if we keep thinking that we can't achieve a goal, our subconscious will help us NOT achieve it.

Second, your reticular activating system cannot distinguish between 'real events' and 'synthetic' reality. In other words it tends to believe whatever message you give it. Imagine that you're going to be giving a speech. You can practice giving that speech by visualizing it in your mind.

What we need to do is to create a very specific picture of our goal in our conscious mind. The RAS will then pass this on to our subconscious - which will then help us achieve the goal. It does this by bringing to our attention all the relevant information which otherwise might have remained as 'background noise'.

The reason psycho cybernetics is so important is that the RAS will prevent our goals messages getting through to our subconscious if our self-image is not congruent with our goals.

Did You Know That Meditating Just 15 Min a Day Could Change Your Life...

Life's Wonders

SENIORS OHAHA

Mind Control

You only need to believe in yourself, nothing else no other requirements, no qualifications just you and your brain. So quit wasting your time take 15 minutes every day and just think. Stop and teach yourself to think. Take another 15 minutes and just relax. Re-program yourself to use the right side of your brain to assist your left brain in everything you think and do.

Command it now simply say to yourself with every breath you take you will feel more in control, More relaxed, feeling better and better than you have ever felt before happier and in perfect health. Your brain can not tell the difference between Imagination and Visualization it just does what you tell it to, and tie it each and breath you take

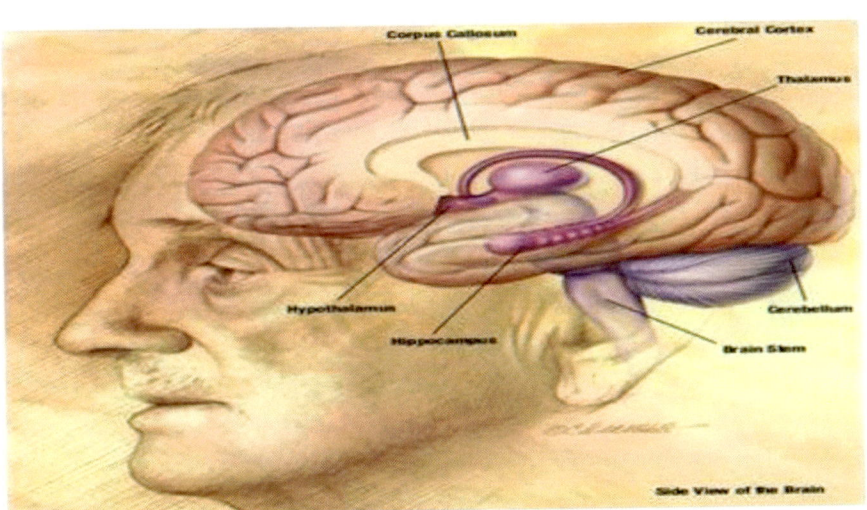

Life's Wonders

Controlled Motivation
Mind Control
Mind Over Matter

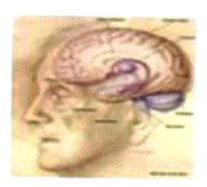

An important aspect of motivation concerns the **energization** of people's psychological processes and behaviors. Within, the energy for action comes either directly or indirectly from basic psychological needs, and we have been particularly interested in the concept of *vitality*, which is the energy that is available to the self—that is, the energy that is exhilarating and persist more at important activities.

Healing is used as a tool for personal and spiritual growth. Many of its users are quick to affirm its profound impact on their mental, emotional and physical well being. self-healing techniques in the therapy.

These techniques are utilized in conjunction with the work to enhance balance in body, mind and spirit. This unique system enables an individual or group, dedicated to helping themselves and others, to offer a procedure simple enough for the average person to learn, yet powerful and in depth, that may be utilized on a daily basis to help bring and maintain optimum health and well being in body, mind and spirit.

The basic teaching of Energy Healing is that all imbalance, pain, illness, etc. that an individual experiences is a direct result of awareness of the Body, Mind and Spirit. Within each one of us, there exists a perfect blueprint of this .

Life's Wonders

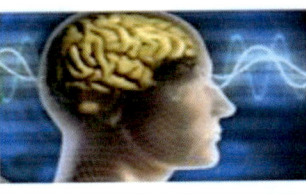 **Dream State**
Live in
Your Dreams

SENIORS OHAHA
Body, Mind & Spirit

It's not hard to be who you are, It's believing in who you are!

The fun part is you can be who ever you want to be,
Understanding you are who you believe yourself to be.

Designed to help you attract everything from wealth, love
Success, loose weight, learn things, understand your
universe and your place in it. The **Mind** will enable you into
entering your Subconscious mind and program all the beliefs
and behaviors that are essential to achieve any thing from
Financial, Health, love, any Success and Fitness. Create
Harmony, good feelings and relationships, Keep excited and
build yourself physically and mentally with the power to
transform and direct your life the direction you wish it to be.

Believing in yourself is the key to Happiness, Faith and
the center of your universe... If God can believe in you so
can you.

You were made to the image and likeness of the GOD
and he only asks that you believe. Believe in yourself.

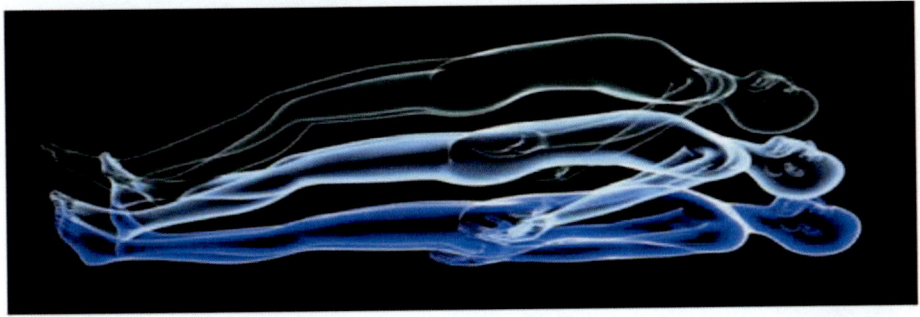

Life's Wonders

LIFE'S WONDERS

SENIORS OHAHA
Control Vibrations, Rhyme

Vibrations when you hear a romantic song the vibrations that you feel brings a smile and loving feeling in your heart and soul. And when you hold or see your baby for the first time, Pride Safety and Security to hold and protect your child. And when you get that tickle in your heart and tummy of pride And happiness when your child says to you I **love you Mom** or I **love you dad**.

The power, strength and honor transfers into Vibration a feeling

That grows in you like a breath of fresh air. Power that you can call up or recall to your use at anytime, anywhere, and place. By changing your vibrations you can do anything , you now at will can change your vibration and create happiness, success, attitude and use this power to complete anything you wish. You want to be happy, or Loving or smarter, creative, romantic, stronger, smarter, more relaxed, you can do anything you wish Just change your vibration at will and make it happen.

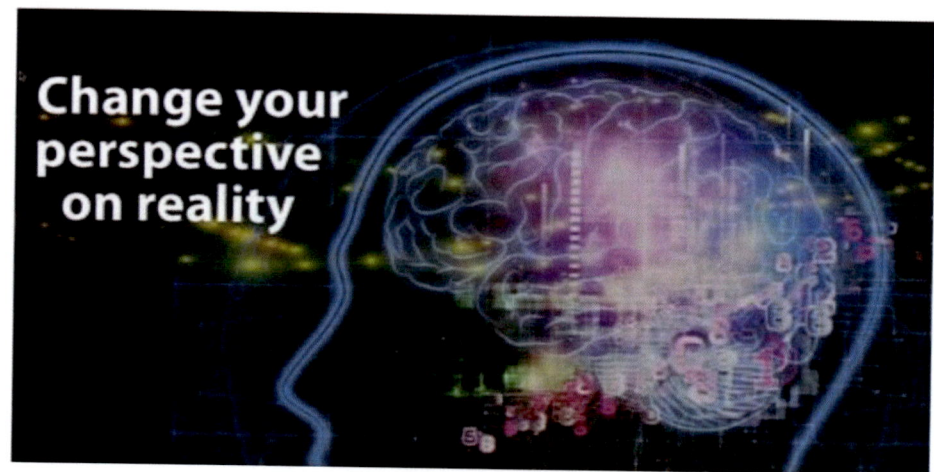

Change your perspective on reality

Life's Wonders

SENIORS OHAHA

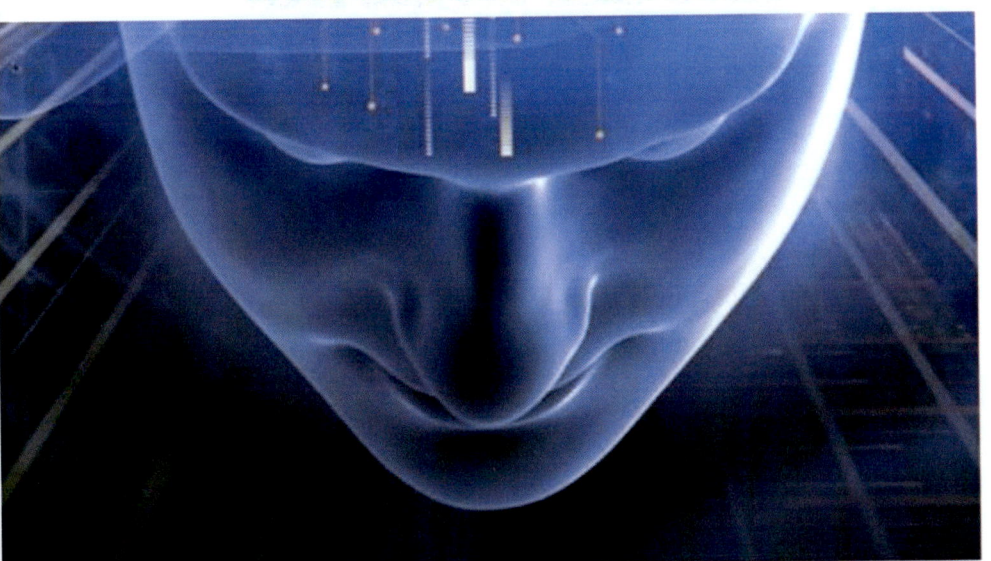

Einstein Explored
Time and Space.

Elbert Einstein asks:

1. Do you feel what you think?
2. Do you see what you fell?
3. Can you hear what you see?
4. See yourself in what you think?
5. Mind over Matter it's all about you!

"The greatest scientists are artists as well," said Albert Einstein As one of the greatest physicists of all time and a fine amateur pianist and violinist, he ought to have known! So what did Einstein mean and what does it tell us about the nature of creative thinking and how we should stimulate it?

Life's Wonders

LIFE'S WONDERS

Einstein explored Time and Space It's a Free trip Do you want to go?

How Much Do You want to Know?

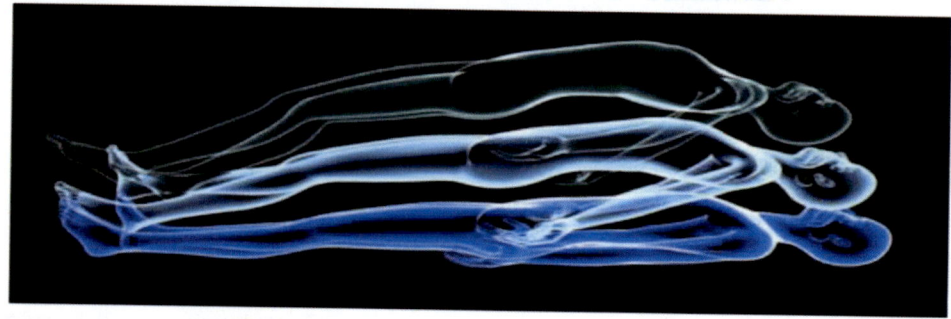

Einstein and Relativity; Out of Body experiences
As we know it's not the findings. It's all that we discover
on the way while we **search time and space** for answers.

Einstein explicated this bold idea at length to one scholar of
creativity in 1959, telling Max Wertheimer that he never
thought in logical symbols or mathematical equations, but
in images, feelings, and even musical architectures
Einstein's autobiographical notes reflect the same thought:
"I have no doubt that our thinking goes on for the most part
without the use of symbols, and, furthermore, largely
unconsciously""

Life is absolutely fun taking a short trip from time to time, in
time. The amount of time is **simply space in time**. Therefore
the time, distance and effort is continuum. Einstein only
employed words or other symbols (presumably
mathematical) -- in what he explicitly called a secondary
translation step -- *after* he was able to solve his problems
through the formal manipulation of internally imagined
images, feelings, and architectures. "I very rarely think in
words at all. **A thought comes in imagined visualization,
and I may try to express it in words** *afterwards*,"

Life's Wonders

LIFE'S WONDERS

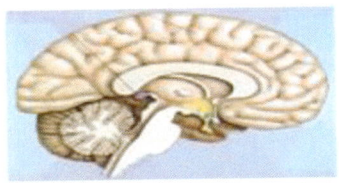 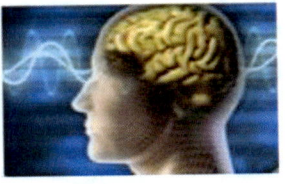 

Brainwave Vibration

- Understanding Brainwaves are simply Vibrations!
- You generate vibrations in every thing you do!
- In your mother woom before you were born!
- A child learning, feeling, seeing, touching the first time!
- As a youth introduction of animals other people!
- During life music, dancing, swimming, running, exercise.
- There are millions of vibrations that make and move you!
- Create your own vibrations, Your Expression.
- Feel, See, Taste, Touch, Hear, Move, Think it's vibrations.
- Smile, Imagine, Remember, Laugh, Cry, vibrations.
- These millions Vibrations help you get through life!

Understanding Vibrations will give you everything you want in life You create happiness, joy, excitement, energy, sadness, fear every Thing in your life is in your control in your power.

Your **Conscious Mind generates** only 40 cycles per second. Your **Sub-Conscious Mind generates** 40 billion cycles per second.
Wow! That means that your **Conscious Mind** leads the way in your Daily life, so Your **Sub-Conscious Mind** can concentrate on keeping you alive and the millions of Voluntary and involuntary functions are always there for you to live and learn new things at the same time. That's why you need to feel what you see, see what you hear, hear what taste, understand that you use all of your senses to expand your power, knowledge and awareness. **Simply Vibrate!!!**

Life's Wonders

LIFE'S WONDERS

BrainWaves
Brainwave Vibration

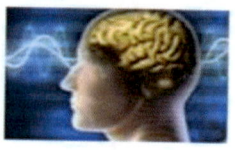

So use this knowledge to reprogram yourself to do or be anything you wish to be or do. Remember Energy can not be created no destroyed! It simply is rearranged based on what and how you wish to see it! Use it, direct it, feel it, taste it and or even except it.

Remember Negative vibrations is the ability to put your brain on hold. Don't get caught with a negative thought.

Also your **breathing and vision** is basis your understanding! Breath correctly and use it to introduce your body to relaxation and Control of effort and your attitude is primary. Vision as you may have heard the phrase **inter minds eye!** Well by using you mind to remember or imagine things and vibrations you are in direct control of your universe, your body and mind. This creates Health, strength, and all the controls you need to function properly.

When we meditate several important things happen physically and mentally. First, we are "focusing internally" and letting go of the outside world (similar to going to sleep, but without losing your consciousness). This allows our brains to shift into more stable, stronger brain frequencies (called alpha and theta by scientists) normally reached during sleep. When we can reduce our brain frequencies to these levels while staying awake we are able to bring the unconscious mind to the conscious level.

You will learn how to reprogram your Conscious mind And teach your Sub-Conscious mind to assist & support.

Life's Wonders

LIFE'S WONDERS

BrainWaves
Brainwave Vibration

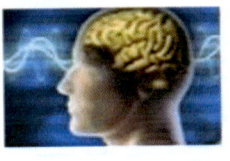 

But what exactly happens when you meditate

You are probably at this beta level of mind right now as you read this. When you go to sleep, your brain frequency slows down, all the way to about half cycle per second in the deepest levels of natural sleep. This is known as the Delta level.

In between Beta, the waking state, and Delta, the deep sleep state, there are two other levels of mental activity. When you are in a light level of sleep or in meditation you are in the Alpha range, which is 7 to 14 cycles per second. This is the center range and this is what we mean by saying **"going to your center"**. Going to the alpha level or centering is essentially the same thing as meditating. When someone meditates, scientifically, they are simply reducing their brain wave frequency to Alpha. The Alpha level is the level we use to activate our minds. Theta is a level of deeper relaxation or sleep, when your brain waves are at 4 to 7 cycles per second. The table below summarizes the 4 states of brain frequency. The vibrations slow down.

STATE	Brain Wave Frequency	Associated with
Beta	14-21 cycles per sec. and higher.	Walking state, the five senses Perception of time and space.
Alpha Meditation, intuition limitation.	7-14 cps	Light sleep, No time and Space
Theta Meditation.	4-7 cps Delta 0-4 cps	Deeper Sleep, Deep Sleep or unconscious at Delta state.

Life's Wonders

BrainWaves
Brainwave Vibration

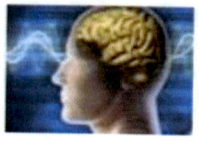

But what exactly happens when you meditate
continued.

There are many benefits of "going to the Alpha level" or meditating. We found that people who can remain in the Alpha level while analyzing information have access to more information than those who remain in Beta to do their thinking. Feelings of intuition, creative ideas, inspirational thoughts and ideas come to people while at this Alpha level. Going to Alpha is also good for programming your mind. At the Alpha level you can learn to overcome all kinds of problems, such as insomnia, tension and migraine headaches, bad habits, and much more. You can also program your mind to help you achieve your goals and make your dreams come true. During the 25 minutes you remain at Alpha while using the your Centering Exercise, you can practice relaxing physically and mentally, and you can imagine yourself succeeding in your projects and achieving your goals. As you can see, there are a lot of benefits to "going to Alpha".

- ☐ reduce stress
- ☐ positively influence your health
- ☐ mentally program yourself to change your attitudes
- ☐ kick bad habits
- ☐ practice creative visualization for goal setting enhance creativity, intuition You can experience this powerful relaxation technique right this instant through your mind.

Life's Wonders

LIFE'S WONDERS

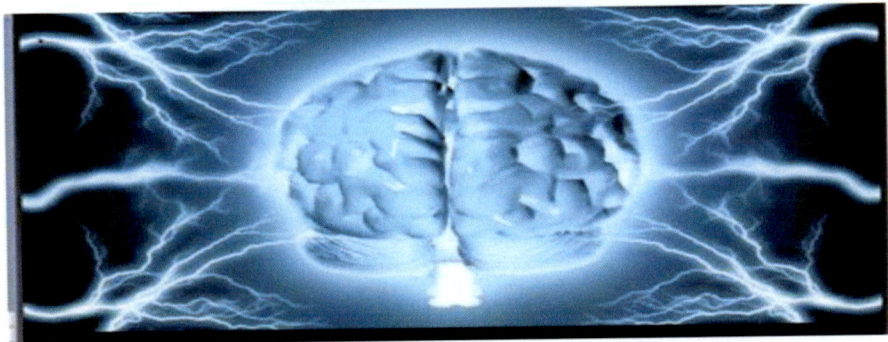

BrainWaves   Brainwave Vibration

Reach Deep Levels of Meditation

FIRST, YOU SHOULD PRACTICE YOUR CONCENTRATION. CONCENTRATION IS A BASIC SKILL.

SECOND, PRACTICE YOUR IMAGINATION. WE WANT YOU TO LEARN HOW TO EXAGGERATE YOUR IMAGINATION, BECAUSE YOU WILL BE IN A BETTER POSITION TO CONTROL YOUR CREATIVE VISUALIZATION. AT THE SAME TIME, IT WILL KEEP YOU ACTIVE WHILE GOING THROUGH THE EXERCISE. BY BEING MENTALLY ACTIVE, YOU AVOID THE TENDENCY TO DRIFT OFF INTO SLEEP.

THIRD, YOU MUST PRACTICE COORDINATING YOUR PHYSIOLOGICAL RELAXATION WITH YOUR MENTAL RELAXATION. IT IS EASY TO GO INTO A MENTAL RELAXATION. BUT YOU MUST LEARN TO LET YOUR BODY RELAX TOO. IT TAKES A LITTLE LONGER FOR YOU TO RELAX YOUR BODY THAN IT DOES FOR YOU TO RELAX YOUR MIND.

YOU DO NOT HAVE TO MAINTAIN A FIXED, RIGID POSITION. IF YOU HAVE TO ADJUST YOUR BODY TO BE COMFORTABLE, DO SO. IF YOU NEED TO SCRATCH AN ITCH, DO IT. MAKE YOURSELF COMFORTABLE AND YOU WILL BE ABLE TO RELAX BETTER. IF YOU FEEL UNCOMFORTABLE FOR ANY REASON, IF YOU FEEL THAT YOU WANT TO OPEN YOUR EYES, THEN OPEN YOUR EYES IMMEDIATELY. TELL YOURSELF—MENTALLY OR VERBALLY— TO RELAX, THAT EVERYTHING IS OKAY.

I will show you step by step how!

Life's Wonders

The Secrets of a Healthier more Enjoyable Life.

Seniors Ohaha Take a quick peek.

➤ *It's Time for You to learn to heal yourself and others!*

Get a copy of Seniors Ohaha for your yourself or Mom and Dad, your Grand Parents, Uncles and Aunties, friends and anyone that is fighting Cancer or Heart *disease or patients recovery.*

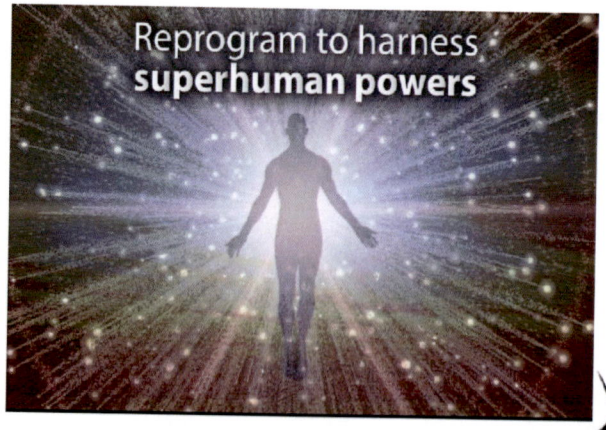

Life's Wonders

Brain Power

Brain Power tied to Universal Power

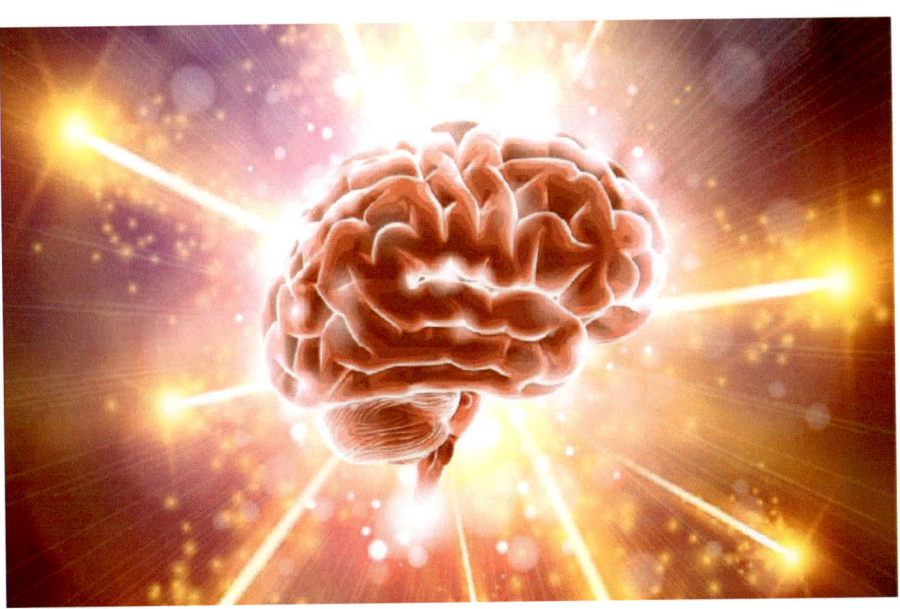

Mind
exercise

Life's Wonders

LIFE'S WONDERS

Life's Wonders

Lifestyles

Things to Know Only Kings, Queens and Gods were allowed to carry the Ankh symbol. The Ankh is the Egyptian sign of life and indicates that the King or God holding it has the power to give life or take it away from lesser mortals. The Ankh is a symbol of the life giving elements of air and water. A God or Goddess would hold the Ankh before the King's nose, giving him the "breath of life" or as streams of water in the form of Ankhs running over the King during ritual purification. The Ankh was a scepter that was popular for Gods to hold, it became a symbol of well-being and happiness for 5000 years.

LIFE'S WONDERS

Choices

SENIORS OHAHA

Heart

Seniors

Seniors Ohaha

SENIORS OHAHA

Cancer

an Ancient Chinese Art of Breathing, Living, Self Healing. Awaken Relaxed and Recharged, Eliminate Pain and Stiffness. Gain Better Range of Motion and Flexibility, Strengthen Your Physical and Mental Control, Return Your Self Confidence and Live a Happier Enjoyable Life

SENIORS OHAHA

PTSD

SENIORS OHAHA

Quad & Para

Seniors Omaha The Secrets of a healthier more enjoyable life.

Life's Wonders

LIFE'S WONDERS

SENIORS OHAHA
Body, Mind & Spirit

SENIORS, CANCER, HEART, PTSD

Use both Right and Left sides of your Brian discover true mental and physical power, your health, wellness, and balance. Become a genius Over night   "Try it you will like it!

Life's Wonders

We are such highly Sophisticated Beings

Remember meditation is not something you want to do in a hurry, the idea is to be relaxed and calm. Your breathing doesn't have to match second for second it merely needs to be continuous like the flow of water. Don't try to count the drops of going through your mind or fingers you will miss the point and splendor of it. Simple embrace the simplicity of its nature, flow and erythematic nature.

Synergy, Mentally, Emotionally, Physically, Health & Wellness, Metaphysically, Philosophically, Promote Awareness, Promote Physical Activity, Promote Physical Strength, Promotes drive, Motivational Awareness.

The Power of your Heart

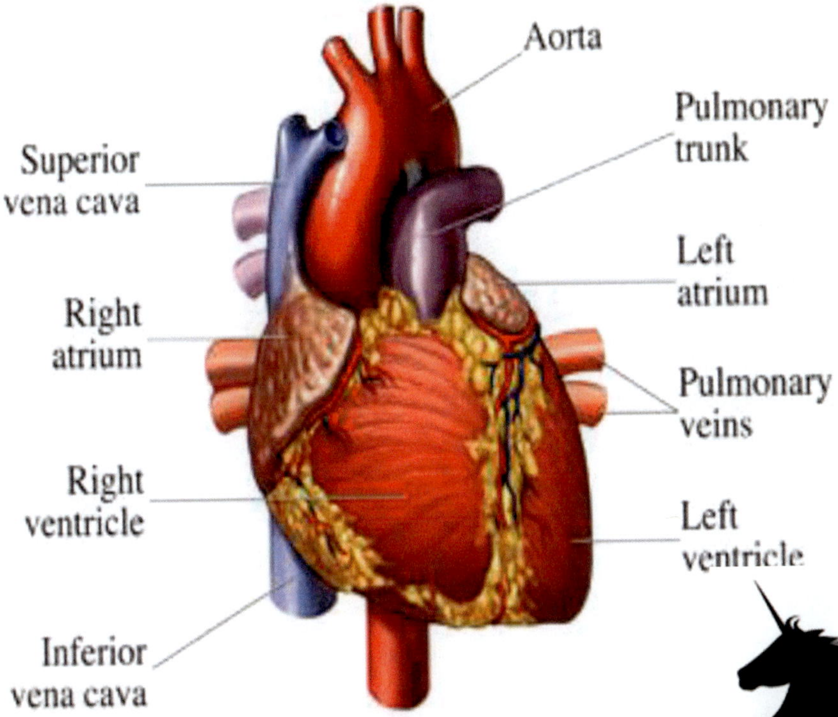

Aorta

Pulmonary trunk

Superior vena cava

Left atrium

Right atrium

Pulmonary veins

Right ventricle

Left ventricle

Inferior vena cava

Life's Wonders

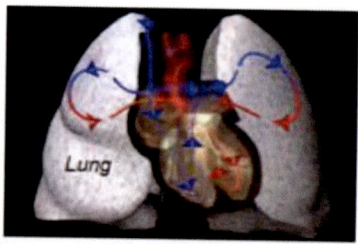

Lungs

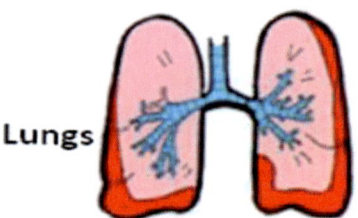

Lungs

Heart, Lungs, Brain, Electrical and Circulation system they all need Blood and Oxygen

Veins carry oxygen-depleted blood (blue) from the body to the heart, which pumps it to the lungs. The lungs enrich the blood with oxygen (red) and return it to the heart to be pumped to the rest of the body. Blood and Oxygen is a must for the entire body. They travel through the digestive area including the intestines, stomach, pancreas, and gall bladder passes through the liver for cleansing and storing of nutrients. This function is often overlooked as critical to the overall circulatory system. Blood flows to the rest of the body including the extremities. Major arteries and veins supplying the arms. Unimpeded circulation of blood to the arteries and veins and from the brain is critical to health Breathing is a must to preventing blockages in the arteries and veins.

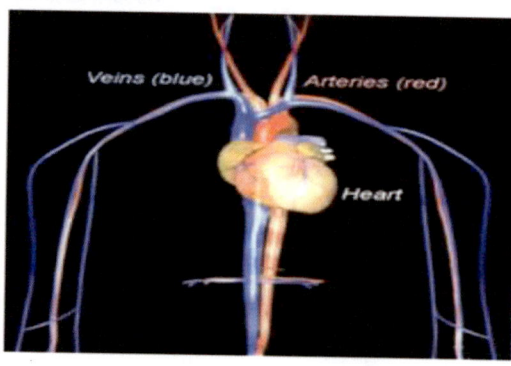

CIRCULATION

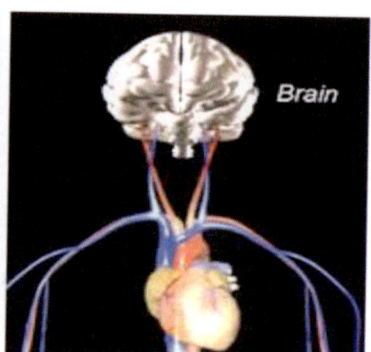

* NEUROLOGICAL

Life's Wonders

SENIORS OHAHA

SENIORS OHAHA
Body, Mind & Spirit

Heart, Lungs, Brain, Electrical, Circulation, system they all need Blood and Oxygen

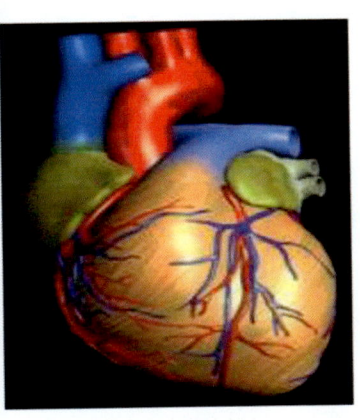

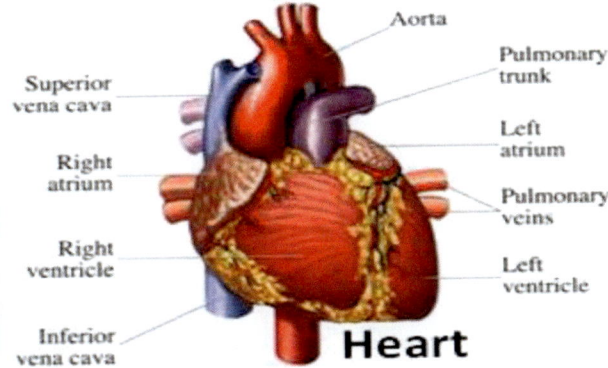

Aorta

Pulmonary trunk

Superior vena cava

Left atrium

Right atrium

Pulmonary veins

Right ventricle

Left ventricle

Inferior vena cava

Heart

Benefits of Seniors Ohaha

- ➤ Psychological and Social Issues
- ➤ Therapy, Restores balance and flexibility
- ➤ Prevent and Control High Blood Pressure
- ➤ Range of motion flexibility eliminate pain
- ➤ Builds positive attitude, Lower your stress
- ➤ Heart, Cancer and medical surgery Recovery
- ➤ Improve mental health, Helping aging process
- ➤ Maintain the movement of your muscles and joints
- ➤ Weight loss and control, Age Healthier, Breathe Easier
- ➤ Sleep better and Awaken recharged, Improve memory
- ➤ Better Nutrition and digestive systems Prevent injuries
- ➤ Exercise, strengthen your entire body, Improve awareness
- ➤ Improve circulation electrical impulse Prevent stiffness

Life's Wonders

LIFE'S WONDERS

SENIORS OHAHA

SENIORS OHAHA
Body, Mind & Spirit

If your having Problems Meditating or getting to Alpha State use the Silva metl

3 to 1 count do.....

This will relax you and put you into a Alfa and Bata state of

mind. Take a deep breath and as you exhale visualize and say

3   **333**

2   **222**

1   **111**

10 to 1 count down or use the Universal Method it's wonderful as well.

9

8

7

6

Once you're at the Alpha Level, the Alpha Exercise will then move on to programming your mind with suggestions and imagery to aid you in visualizing an encounter with your alternate self.

5

4

3

2

Alpha Exercises are visually, mentally and spiritually engaging.

1

They're deep, relaxing and enjoyable experiences that last between 30 minutes to an hour per session.

Life's Wonders

LIFE'S WONDERS

SENIORS OHAHA

Energy Healing and Control

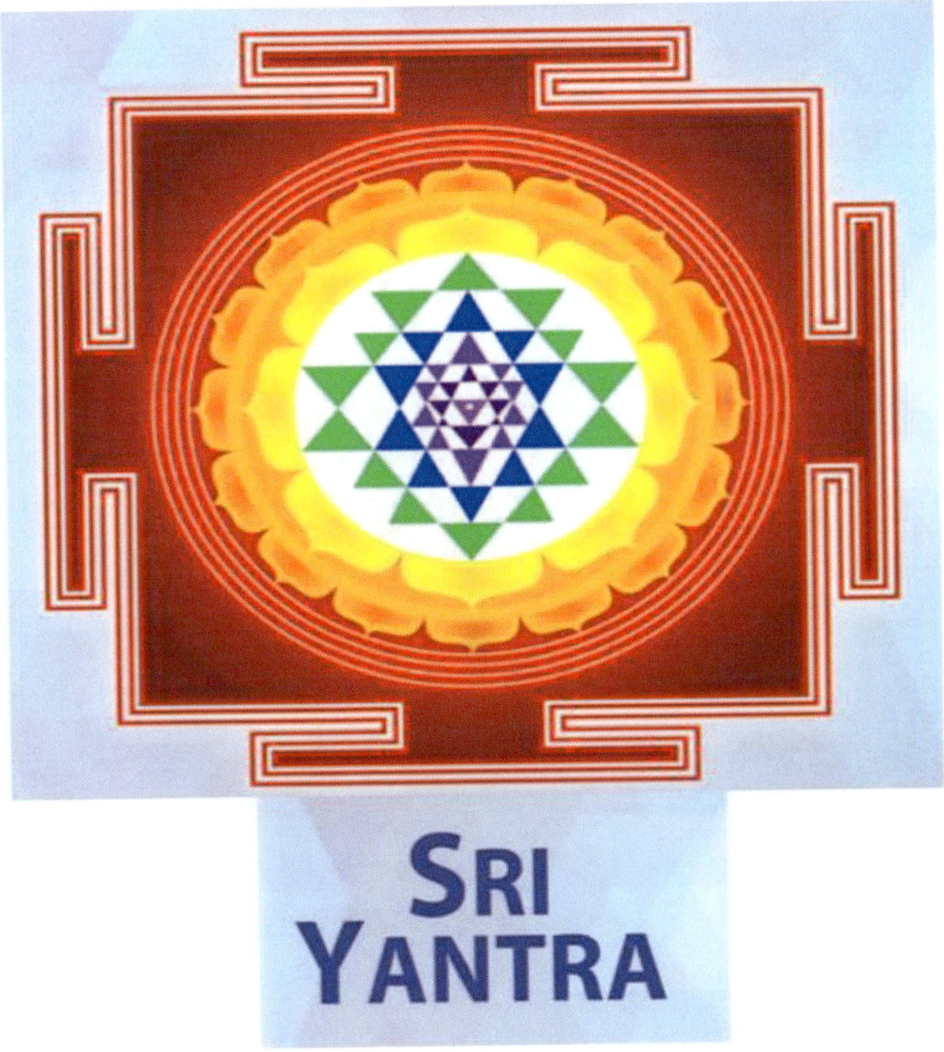

SRI YANTRA

Sri Yantra is a road map to the Universe

Life's Wonders

SENIORS OHAHA

Control Vibrations, Rhyme
It's all about you!

Belief
Is to
Know
Oneself
To
Know
Oneself
Is to
Believe
In
Yourself!

Look and you will feel,
Feel and you will see
See and you will hear,
Hear and you will know
Know and you will believe,
Reach out and touch your
Universe....

Simply change and Understand your Vibrations

Life's Wonders

SENIORS OHAHA

Seniors Ohaha *is an Ancient Chinese Art of Breathing and Living combined with the Chinese art of Tai Chi Kung-Fu exercise. It helps people regain flexibility, strength, range of motion, better digestive systems, sleep better and awaken recharged, strengthen mind control and so much more. Take control of your life again. This is a journey of knowledge, experience and secrets of life for the young of all ages. It's mind over mater take control of oneself. Turn negative into positive, by taking control of your fear,. By this simple and easy process of learning to breath correctly a person can strength their mental, spiritual and physical well being by something that is so simple and yet so powerful.*

Life's Wonders

LIFE'S WONDERS

Welcome to **Seniors Ohaha!**
My Name is **Professor Michael Sandos**

Seniors Ohaha is an Ancient Chinese Art of Breathing and Living combined with Chinese art of Tai Chi Kung-Fu exercise. It helps people regain flexibility, strength, range of motion, Better digestive systems, sleep better and awaken recharged, Strengthen mind control and so much more. This is a journey of knowledge, experience and secrets of life for the young of all ages. In fact you will laugh and giggle in memories of knowing this in your life.

Simply Said: Its Mind over Matter, Called **Controlled Motivation** Turn **Negative** into **Positive**, by taking control of your fear, By this simple and easy process of **learning to breath correctly** a person can strength their **Mental, Spiritual and Physical** well being by something that is so simple and yet so powerful. **Yes,** as you already know **Controlled Motivation is the most difficult thing to do in the world.**

I will show you how to do this in a simple and easy way! We have this in the Martial Arts for thousands of years. No matter what triggers **Stress, Illness, Death,** loss of a loved one, or a job, I will show you how to turn that **negative** into **Positive.**

3 simple things;
#1. Simply breathing; take 7 breaths 7 times
    Inhale through your nose, Exhale out your mouth
#2. Mind Control; Reprogram your **Conscious mind** to
    Direct the **Sub conscious mind** to do this naturally **24-7**
#3. Low impact Tia Chi Exercise, Internal motion and
    Understanding of how this works.

Life's Wonders

LIFE'S WONDERS

SENIORS OHAHA

禄喜寿

SENIORS OHAHA

Science discovers how Tai Chi works

Scientist have discovered why this ancient art with a simple Set of exercises provides such healing benefits to the body. Traditional exercise helps us to loose weight and build muscle. Whenever we exercise, our bodies produces chemicals that are not produced when we are still.

Most exercise causes the body to damage some muscle. When this is repaired the muscle grows back stronger. The chemicals produced by the body is the medicine that allows the muscle to heal. When Tai Chi is practiced, the movements are so gentle that muscle isn't damaged. However, the body still produces the same chemicals as it does during normal exercise. Since there is no damaged muscle that needs healing, the healing chemicals can be utilized by the other parts of the body. Our bodies produce the very medicine needed to heal itself. Normal exercise produces them and uses them up.

Tai Chi releases the healing chemicals but doesn't use them up. Another important ingredient in Tai Chi is the utilization of oxygen's ability to heal. During normal exercise we breathe hard and increase our intake of oxygen. The hard work causes cells in the muscles to become oxygen starved. The deep breathing provides the needed healing oxygen. Part of Tai Chi practice is to breathe deeply and slowly while performing the gentle movements. The same principle again applies. The deep breathing provides more oxygen than the muscles need. The extra oxygen is available to the other cells. This also helps the heart, brain and other organs to receive a double dose of oxygen and the healing chemicals, increasing the healing power of both.

Life's Wonders

LIFE'S WONDERS

SENIORS OHAHA **is an Ancient** *Chinese Art of Breathing and Living combined with the Chinese art of Tai Chi Kung-Fu exercise. It helps people regain flexibility, strength, range of motion, better digestive systems, sleep better and awaken recharged, strengthen mind control and so much more. Take control of your life again. This is a journey of knowledge, experience and secrets of life for the young of all ages. Its mind over matter take control of oneself. Turn negative into positive, by taking control of your fear, By this simple and easy process of learning to breath correctly a person can strength their mental, spiritual and physical well being by something that is so simple and yet so powerful. Different chants for different objectives these are examples of, but try not to be to critical of things and yourself let yourself have room to grow! These are connectional formats once you program yourself to them they are very much automatic.*

Modern life is filled with stress and tension, Tai Chi can be a powerful effective alternative to an all-too-common reliance on prescription drugs or cocktails after work.

Master Sandos goes on to explain that this time-honored, slow motion form of exercise can unblock acupuncture channels, known as "meridians," and create relaxation naturally so that the "chi" or life energy will flow naturally, improving concentration, circulation, and the tone of the nervous system. Master Sandos says that these benefits mean a stronger immune system, better physical fitness, and better health in general. "If we are stressed, "our energy will be restricted. If you are relaxed you will create more peace more harmony and more balance in your life. That's true! Tai Chi will give you a more peaceful mind and stronger body."

Life's Wonders

LIFE'S WONDERS

Study: Tai Chi is Heart Healthy

Life's Wonders

group of Chinese elders spread out along the lower East River bike path in Manhattan
practice a gentle, flowing martial arts form known as Tai Chi.

Every morning, rain or shine, a group of Chinese elders spread out along the lower East River bike path in Manhattan to practice a gentle, flowing martial arts form known as Tai Chi. Their body motions are so slow and deliberate it almost looks as if they're moving underwater. They don't pound the pavement, burn a lot of calories or pump any iron yet the science shows they may be doing just as much for their health as the joggers and cyclists who zip past them. The latest evidence looking into the health benefits of Tai Chi comes from researchers at Beth Israel Deaconess Medical Center and Harvard Medical School in Boston, who followed a group of heart failure patients as they took a twice weekly Tai Chi class for three months. At the end of the study -- published in today's Archives of Internal Medicine, one of the JAMA/Archives journals -- the Tai Chi practitioners felt better, were more confident about their ability to perform everyday tasks and led far more active lifestyles than a similar group who attended twice-weekly health education classes.

The subjects in this most recent study didn't increase aerobic fitness levels but in previous studies where subjects attended class more often and practiced a more strenuous version of Tai Chi, they did. Other studies found Tai Chi helps build bone density, lower blood pressure and even boost the immune system, physical benefits normally attributed exclusively to more vigorous workouts. Dr. Gloria Y. Yeh, the lead author of the study, says that judging Tai Chi exclusively on its physical advantages. In her opinion one of their most striking findings is that the martial artists stuck with the plan; more than three quarters of them kept up their practice the entire 12 weeks and many were still at it when the researchers checked up on them six months later. Considering that less than two-thirds of American adults are physically active on a regular basis and a quarter get virtually no exercise, Yeh thinks Tai Chi can serve as an ideal bridge into a more active lifestyle. "We know one of the biggest assets of any exercise regimen is adherence. This makes accessibility one of Tai Chi's most valuable components," she says.

A Martial Art for All Walks Of Life

What makes Tai Chi so appealing, especially to the over-50 crowd, is that it combines slow movements and stationary postures with breathing techniques and mental focus to create a soothing yet invigorating effect. Although technically considered a martial art, it's more for those interested in fighting their internal demons rather than outside attackers.

"I started because I was looking for healing and stress release and the gym wasn't really for me," says William, a 61-year-old former manager who been taking Tai Chi for three years at Tao Yoga, a tiny studio tucked inside an office building off Union Square. "It definitely clears my mind and helps me get in touch with my true self."

Kathy, 55, a food writer, agrees. She realized she needed to do something to get in shape but she accepted the fact that she was never going to be a gym rat. Now she attends the milder class taught at Tao Yoga several times a week as well as a more vigorous class taught in Chinatown. "I feel lightness in my body and can breathe more fully since I started three months ago. I definitely have more flexibility, strength and balance too," she says.

But Tai Chi certainly isn't the exclusive domain of Golden Agers. More than 7 million Americans age 6 and older participated in yoga or Tai Chi classes last year, reports the Sporting Goods Manufacturers Association (SGMA), a 16 percent increase over 1999, and a 30 percent jump over 1998 figures. The average class taker is female and 40 years old.

Some hardcore fitness buffs use it as an antidote to stress and to buffer their more high-impact activities. Instructor Shavon Schwartz says her classes are often filled with 20- and 30y-something males who want to feel calmer and more grounded. "Older people may do it to ease arthritis pain but everyone has their own reason for showing up."

Life's Wonders

LIFE'S WONDERS

 # SENIORS OHAHA

By learning to breathe correctly, a person can create and control their state of mind and conquer the challenges in their lives.

Be a Seniors Ohaha Black Belt and join the Battle Against Cancer, Heart Disease, PTSD for our Vet's and all medical recovery patients. *Martial Artists Battle Against Heart & Cancer Disease*

Seniors Ohaha is very close to my heart. I am a Master in the Chinese Art of Kung-Fu Mixed Martial Arts and live in Utah. I am a veteran of the Vietnam War and know what it's like to lay in a hospital bed hoping to see my family again; looking for strength to recover and enjoy life again

Seniors Ohaha, has helped so many people as well as myself and has given me the opportunity to teach others. To see the passion of an individual with a heart condition or a cancer patient feeling like there is something to live for is so gratifying. It's so hard when the loss of life or health issues have threatened you or your family. It's time to fight back!

Seniors Ohaha is specifically designed for Seniors, Cancer, Heart and all medical recovery patience. We have a wonderful responsibility to help, teach, understand and provide a second chance for folks when they have had either _life_ or _time_ taken away from them. They need to recover and take back the controls of life that is so deeply needed. I would be honored to have you and your organization join me in presenting this wonderful opportunity.

Life's Wonders

LIFE'S WONDERS

SENIORS OHAHA

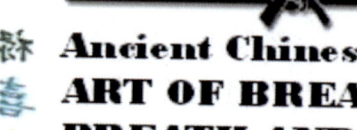 Ancient Chinese Secret
ART OF BREATHING
BREATH AND LIVE

Understandings
Breath of Life

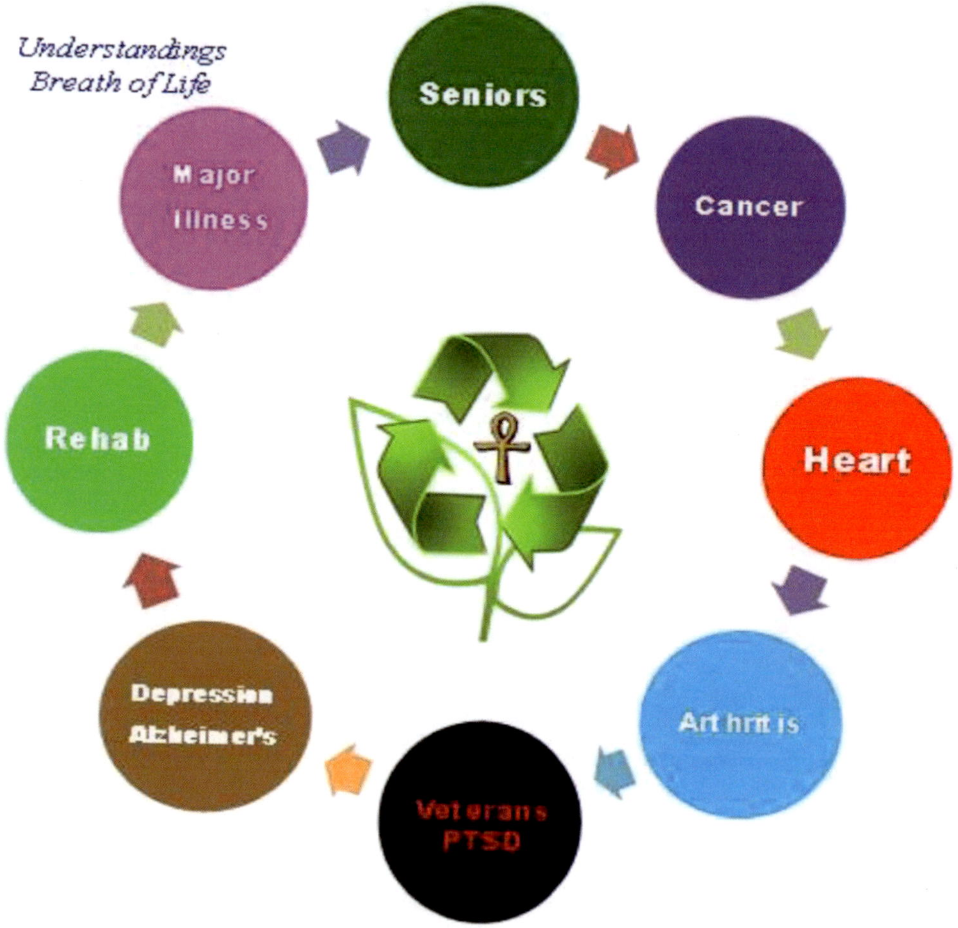

Seniors

Cancer

Major Illness

Heart

Rehab

Arthritis

Depression Alzheimer's

Veterans PTSD

Life's Wonders

LIFE'S WONDERS

SENIORS OHAHA

Purpose

Seniors Ohaha will teach you how to take control of your body and mind. The main problem is how we react to the changes in our lives. Don't let negative changes and things in your life turn into stress and then takes over. Most of the time people don't understand that it's themselves that let negativity over-come their lives and thoughts. They are actually making those negative things turn into reality. It's your choice take control and turn the negative into positive. It doesn't matter what triggers stress, Illness, death, loss of a job. whatever it may be, that may cause it, by simply breathing correctly and through relaxed meditation, mind control you can change that negative power and turn it back into a positive power.

The problem begins in how we react to stress. We don't notice the changes that are taking place in our lives. Many things can happen from loss of control, diet, loss of sleep, physical changes, a lack of exercise or by your thoughts and reactions and responses. These are signs that your body gives you to let you know something is wrong. We can't let fear take over, instead we need to relax and make the changes you need to by taking control again of your life. You must relax, take a deep breath feel a sense of calm confidence as you feel yourself relax. You will learn to understand and believe in yourself that the controlled motivation you will learn herein will return you and your life back to your control. You must understand you already have all the tools to do this. God gave you all that you will need to correct this and take control of your life again. Your body is just giving you warnings signs that these things are taking place.

Life's Wonders

SENIORS OHAHA

Purpose

You simply need to listen and respond. You must not get angry or afraid. These warning signs are a natural process that the body does to try to protect us. We simple need to take control and stay calm relaxed. Remember that one of the best and most powerful way to react is to smile, your smile will automatically start to calm you and give you the power. By practicing this you are learning to acting and not just react.

*Believe in yourself. Laugh in the face of fear and change. Smile and take a big breath and feel yourself relax and be at peace with yourself. You must believe in yourself, know that no matter what happens that you have the power and you are in control. Even if you say, 'but I really don t know."
But you do know, you see your Conscious mind simple needs you to tell it, to command the subconscious mind to heal and fix your body. You have the tools built in to your body to do this. It will know how and what to do automatically.*

You must understand your mind and body needs you to tell it what to do. Your Conscious mind needs to hear your command and must feel your believe and tell it that it is ok, and it will do the rest for you. Don t forget

Life's Wonders

SENIORS OHAHA

Purpose

Seniors Ohaha *Seniors have a habit of breathing shallow, and not standing straight up, having problem going to sleeping and or staying asleep, you needing to learn how to relax. You need to understand that when you go to bed and ending your day you need to unplug yourself as to say. The word Ohaha to breath! Simply means **Oh = inhale / aha = Exhale** Ohaha to*

Take the time to let your body unwind. Seniors Ohaha shows you how to do that. To get to sleep faster and stay asleep and wake up more recharged. Follow the Senior Ohaha instructions step by step learning how to Physically and mentally take control of your life again. By breathing correctly with a mental and physical collaboration and compliment of ancient Chinese secrets of living.

There are so many people that help us, parents, family, friends and caregivers and they too can use Seniors Ohaha either with us or themselves as well. The fun part is that while they are helping you with your understanding and use of Seniors Ohaha you will be giving back to them something we all need and that is the knowledge and practice of Seniors Ohaha.

Now with all this in mind let's take the next step in understanding the tools that we need and use to make this happen. As I said God has given you everything you will need. You just need to use them and believe in yourself. Now let have some fun.

Life's Wonders

SENIORS OHAHA

Understanding your tools

Seniors Ohaha *It's all about mind control. It's time to be the movie star in your own movie. It's so important that you take control and do it now. For the next few months you must be superman or superwoman, hero or heroine in your life. The next step is to learn to meditate.*

MIND - *The mental healing is all part of correcting the imbalances of your body and mind. It's time to reprogram yourself for an enjoyable and happy life. You will need to learn to relax. Relaxation within the effort is key. Breathe*

BODY — *You need to direct The body, you have all the tools your body needs you to tell it what to do and it will do it.*

SPIRIT - *No matter who you believe in God or the creator or greater power the word is <u>believe,</u> believe in yourself. God has given you the tools already to do the rest.*

EMOTIONS — *Emotions are the toughest thing to deal with. You can't let your emotions take over and push you into panic or stress. Breath deep and simply relax and count on your conscious mind to direct your subconscious mind to command your body to heal and it will. God has bless us all with all the tool for self healing. The Doctors, operations and drugs are tools to help get us back on track. Trust in yourself and you will be pleasantly surprised and happy you did!*

Life's Wonders

SENIORS OHAHA

Process

The fun begins breath and relax, If you fall asleep, that's ok it just means that your body needs to relax more often, and it needs to have more oxygen. Enjoy your sleep and try again later after you have rested. If you fall asleep again that's ok . We need to keep trying until we have built up, and caught up on our rest. Next time we may want to stand or sit comfortably. But don't be in a hurry catch up on your rest and relaxation you will build as your body sees fit. As they say," in our own time and place." Our body gets its food from us when we breathe.

When oxygenating the blood stream our blood starts to circulate a bit faster. The blood goes through the membrane of the mussel and tissue pushing out the old blood and garbage into the blood veins. (Blue Veins) Our blood carries the garbage off so the body can process it to waste.

Whenever your body bruises it's just the old blood that gets smashed against the blood veins. When we allow our blood to circulate it cleans the blood veins and our blood to give us new life and in growth.

Try picturing this process as you breath. See the old blood flow out as you exhale. And Now breath in and see the rich, healthy blood flow in an circulate through your body.

Life's Wonders

LIFE'S WONDERS

SENIORS OHAHA

Note: *When the blood in the veins gets smashed It coagulates and bruises.*
Whenever this happens just rub your hands together and get them hot. Then rub your hands on the bruise semi lightly and in a circular motion. What you are doing is helping the blood that is smashed and bruised go away. We really should do this before it turns into a bruise. Rub it just as soon as it happens and it will not bruise or coagulate. Notice that not only did the bruise go away, but also you are not tender in that spot any more. Sometimes it takes a couple of times to get it to completely go away! But keep trying don t let it get sore **and turn into a bruise.**

Remember to have some fun when we are traveling through the body. Like any trip see what you can see and do something fun like tapping on the big toe from the inside. Pretend that you are knocking on the toe nail to get out. Let your body tingle and giggle from the reality when you feel and see yourself there. Mentally we need to always be in good communication with ourselves both on a physical and mental basis. All we need to do is tell our body what we want it to do and it will. We can tell it to heal, feel better, fix itself, or grow just about anything we can dream up and it will participate. If you get a little light headed don t worry you are just breathing to fast, slow down and relax. We can travel through our body and do all kinds of things. Once communication is developed the system can deliver any message any where and any time to our body in a split second. Be calm patience's don t worry it will come to you naturally.

Life's Wonders

SENIORS OHAHA

Our Mind's Eye

We can fix things, help things along, heal ourselves and repair things faster. Just by using our **mind's eye**. What does that mean We have such a powerful computer inside us that it has a main hard drive as to say or main control that sees and feels everything, It keeps track of the difference in our thoughts and our mind making requests vs. commands with precise coordinated efficiency.

Example Think of your hand about to touch something cold or hot. The mind anticipates it and the body actually responds to the thought of actually touching it, before you have even touched it. Your computer has already given you and your physical body a command to acknowledge the sensations.

The mind starts to prepare the body to go into a shock mode and to start to react to the action. As we know to every action there is an equal and opposite reaction. Our body starts to secrete moisture in the glands even though we have not even touched the surface yet. The brain communicates back and gives us a communication not to touch it because it will hurt. The mind over rides everything and gives a command to the body to pull away. We need to have our body create more of something so we can safely complete an action without injury. Like a weight lifter takes a bunch of deep breathes and runs thoughts of strength telling all muscles to get ready for a surge, Mentally and physically he aligns them to lift a heavy weight and pressurizes the system to react.

Life's Wonders

SENIORS OHAHA

Now why do we need to know all this? Our system is older and is not running at full capacity. In most cases it never has and now we will be calling on more of our brain cells to work and all of our body functions to participate. Our body has over the years quit producing certain chemicals and systems that are needed to run our body at peak efficiency. We are simply letting our body recreate these functions naturally and safely. We need to allow more of ourselves to participate then ever before to achieve a healthier and happier life. The funny part about it is that it really is easier to do than the way we have been doing it, all our life . We have NOT been communicating with ourselves over all these years.

So get ready were going to have some fun! Your heart is going to smile while we laugh at the simply little things we do that we have been missing out on up to now! The funny part is that we will recognize many things that we had stumbled on during life and forgot about. We are all children of God just relearning all the things we never took the time for, or never made the time for before now! Some could say It's all in our head! Yet others say, how did we walk past so much in life and never noticed it until now. " Don t forget to stop and smell the roses"

Let's take your hands and reach down to the lower front of the body and in a soft circular motion with open hand pull the air back toward your body and in an up ward lifting action while inhaling through the nose. Then exhale through the mouth.

Life's Wonders

SENIORS OHAHA

Understandings your tools

You control Conscious Mind

Your Conscious Mind controls the Sub-Conscious Mind

Your Sub-Conscious Mind controls the body functions

Mind controls **Emotions** as our **Spirit** of beliefs direct

Body to heal, assist, helps our bodies function properly.

Everything about you is an amazing miracle. They each function separately yet have a total dependence of and on each other. Some stop their production or function when another will not or is not able to participate. This is the most beautiful collaboration that you will ever see or experience. We all take our bodies for granite, that it will always be there for us.

Once you understand and see how all this works, you will be in awe. It's like being reborn again and you are in control. You will have a hard time keeping a big grin or a smile off your face. The joy, fun success will over whelm you and you will laugh until it hurts as you realize how simple and easy it was. So sit back and relax, don't get in a hurry simply breath.

As we get started take a deep breath through your nose and exhale through your mouth. While doing that tell your body to relax. Feel your body drop into ezzz as you exhale really let go and release all your body tension.

Life's Wonders

SENIORS OHAHA

Breathing

- If you breath through your nose your lungs fill.
- If you breath through Your mouth your tummy fills.
- Inhale through your nose, Exhale through your mouth

There are 5 different chants or phrases that you will need to say to yourself each and every time you take a breath.

1. With each and every breath I take , I feel so **relaxed**, so much more relaxed than I have ever felt before.

2. With each and every breath I take , I feel so **good**, so much better than I have ever felt before.

3. With each and every breath I take , I feel so **recharged**, so much more recharged than I have ever felt before.

4. With each and every breath I take , I feel so **happy**, so much happier than I have ever felt before.

5. With each and every breath I take , I feel **stronger**, so much stronger than I have ever felt before.

As you get more comfortable with this you will add 5 more chants or phrases of or requests of your own. As an example:

A. With each and every breath I take , I feel **a live**, so much a live than I have ever felt before.

B. With each and every breath I take , I feel **my immune system** working through my body healing, fixing and repairing injuries.

C. With each and every breath I take , I feel **more aware**, so much more aware than I have ever felt before. Add anything like **I need money**, or **I want Knowledgeable**

Life's Wonders

LIFE'S WONDERS

SENIORS OHAHA

SENIORS OHAHA
Body, Mind & Spirit

Breathing

As you begin breathing and saying the chants you are reprogramming yourself. You can tell your mind to make you more receptive to the materials your studying. Let your mind and sub-conscious mind help you translate or understand how things work. It's like studying at school and you're needing help understanding new materials. **But don't forget to breath!**

Things to remember

- *Never be in a* **hurry** *there's plenty of time.*
- *Be* **calm** *move softly in your heart, body and mind.*
- *Remember it's your life* **enjoy** *learning to reprogram.*
- **Share** *your new found knowledge and self confidence.*

One of the best things to chant or phrase to use is that you are totally healed or I am a 100% success, I am a winner.

You see you are what you believe yourself to be if you think your Sick, you will be sick and if you think negative than negative is what you get. It's all about your mind when your body is relaxed you can reprogram to be anything you need whether it's to be healthier, brighter, smarter, happier, wealthy, stronger, recharged anything. Your mind will program your sub-conscious mind to get the job done.

The major problem is people let stress and negative emotions take over and they become negative. They make it happen to themselves, They become what they think about. Change all that, believe in yourself and be positive ... **Simply Breath!**

Life's Wonders

LIFE'S WONDERS

SENIORS OHAHA

SENIORS OHAHA
Body, Mind & Spirit

Learning and Giving

You see we all need each other to learn from
As a child we learned from our parents, teachers, family
and friends. As we grew we found that we learned from
others churches, schools and other organizations until
we had the confidence to believe in ourselves and we
then taught as well. **Learn to share**

As the **Kings and Queens** of time we also found
responsibility to ourselves as well as one another. As We
uncover the secrets of life, part of that responsibility is to
share. To share what we have Learned and found again
with each other. We are kings or queens of our time. We
were blessed with life and we now are the **seniors** how
wonderful it is that. What a great honor you have been
given with this opportunity to share with the youth of
today to and build the youth of tomorrow and leave your
imprint on time. Simply because we understood the
secrets of life. **Simply Breath!**

Remember New Knowledge New things.

Now that you know how to travel try stepping out of your
body and look down at yourself from about 10 to 20 feet
above. Now take a look at your past life and your
present life and see Which direction you wish to go.
Notice the turns you could of made but didn t. Notice the
opportunity for new and more choices. Enjoy your new
found maps of life. Laugh and giggle with a deep breath
and enjoy life you have earned it...

Life's Wonders

LIFE'S WONDERS

SENIORS OHAHA

CONTROLLED MOTIVATION. We will be building your abilities to control the hardest thing ever. "our own motivation" This is called controlled motivation.

Balance Equal and Opposite
With each and every breath that we take from the very first breath that we take to every motion that we do. we will be learning how to program ourselves for success and a healthier happier life. Just the fact of being in more control of our mind and body creates motivation. Understanding gives us great motivation to stay in control and enjoy that relationship.

Remember that we need to reset ourselves both through the mind and body. We need to tell our mind and body to take a break, relax the muscles and mind let everything rest without worry and concerns of the day. We must master the communication within ourselves and feel a relaxed sense of well being and awareness of ones-self. Create an that inner rhythm that will release stress in your mind and body tensions. We must create an inner harmony as well as relaxation while we breathe. This ties everything to the life giving source of breathing. Once you've programmed yourself to tie this to life force breathing, you are assured success. The Ying Yang, shows balance of life. Equal and Opposite, and the Negative and Positive. Create your own life force by continuous motion.

Life's Wonders

SENIORS OHAHA

The Key to Life's success...

Motivation: *This is the most important thing you need to do! Teaching yourself to do the hardest thing in the world there is to do, and that is self motivation.*

This is what makes people winners or losers, success or failure happy or sad, rich or poor, It's the balance of power in your life. This alone will give you more control of your life and give you the success that you deserve and have earned. It will open the doors for you to respect and honor yourself, it will bring your life together. It will fulfill those missing gaps in yourself with total pride and confidence. This is the key to life and you believing in yourself. This is where most fail, and other never even get started. This is so hard for most everyone to do and control. The secret to success by simply breathing!

We will tie this wonderful thing to something so simple and basic. This is something that you do every day of your entire life, and that is breathing! This way you can never miss never forget or fail. You are going to laugh with joy and a smile that will tickle all over your body and mind with complete satisfaction by finally knowing this simple secret. We will tie this to breathing but we need to first teach you how to breath properly. Yes, It's a win, win situation you can t loose by tying this. By breathing your success is guaranteed because you need to breathe everyday all the time to live, so you're assured of success with confidence.

Life's Wonders

SENIORS OHAHA

Motivation

This is one of the most important stage, that you Need to understand totally. We're now going to start reprogramming ourselves to rebuild and repair our body and mind. We are letting our body deliver food and energy, this will repair and clean the body by replacing the old nutriments with new nourishment to our system. We will rebuild the white corpuscles taking new blood to the body replacing and building new enzymes and amino acids. This we generally give our body an over haul with each and every breath we take. In some cases this is the first time we have ever taken control of our system and self.

How fun and wonderful this opportunity is for most of our life is gone, and we're finding out about a great tool that we never knew we had. We have the power to heal, ourselves and have direct control of our body and how we feel.

The sequence and uniformity with collaboration of the Respiratory, Circulatory and Electrical system promotes a healthier relationship within yourself. The inner-mind's eye, the subconscious mind a vision of communication that puts us into a mediation position with our self. Control Note: With a multi-tasking event remember to breath, and let your inner mind's eye command you while we breath, to feel better, happier and recharged all at the same time. Now instruct your body to always participate with us always when breathing. This helps create this action as a natural on going thing. Success is your right of participation.

Life's Wonders

SENIORS OHAHA

Secrets of Circulation and Mind Control

You can control the body and the mind eliminate illness simply by breathing, this will calm the mind, and become absolutely in control. The negative emotion attached to the subconscious is so powerful you need to use the controlled motivation of Seniors Ohaha to control it and direct your conscious and subconscious mind. You can control healing, growth, pain, illness, recovery, mental and physical strengthening .

The power of the mind is incredible . You will be happier and enjoy life just by controlling your mind and it's direction. Many illnesses are suppressed emotion—things that are too painful to feel or acknowledge. Until we access and experience these feelings, all other approaches are only temporary fixes until we address the true causes. To facilitate this, breathing exercises, visualizations, and affirmations are utilized.

Breathing Exercises

The first exercise is breathing, this is to oxygenates the tissues and calms the mind. Breath through the nose and exhale through the mouth. Follow the air path and travel through the body by totally capturing the mind. Spinal support gives balance of energy and supports the controlled motivation of Seniors Ohaha. These breathing exercises reduce the inflammatory response common to major disease, meditation or controlled motivation will bring everything together

Life's Wonders

LIFE'S WONDER

SENIORS OHAHA

Secrets of Circulation and Mind Control

Visualization Exercises

Healing is visualized in the mind which is successively transferring it into the eyes, ears, nose, and mouth. This addresses the senses of sight, hearing, smell and taste. Healing subsequently flows through visualization into the organs, veins and arteries of the circulatory system including the coronary, pulmonary, cerebral, renal, and hepatic portal systems. Healing is mentally traveling through out the body and mind.

3) Affirmations

The correct words need to placed in the subconscious mind to have real power and the correct the real truth and to have corresponding images that give you proper mental control.

Mental rehearsal, you must practice your controlled Motivation you need to think, to see, and let the mind feel what you think and see what you are feeling.

Listen to your tissue and organs feel what they are saying and listen to the blood flow. Support and believe in yourself of what you see, feel and hear. Support healing and direct positive commanding energy with yourself. Tell the conscious and subconscious mind to support and guide you in your understanding and placement of same.

Life's Wonders

SEERIORS OHAHA

Seniors Ohaha puts you back in control ag.
Reduce risks and increases control and directs our
life in the direction that you wish to go. It promotes,
healthy eating, exercise, digestive, weight, physical
activity, heart, diabetes, cancer, chronic diseases, helps
you sleep better, and awaken recharged, It takes away
stiffness and pains, and improves attitude, nutrition, and
your metabolism. It helps with controlling blood pressure,
cholesterol. You will enjoy the fun you will have in doing
all the things you love.

Don't forget to take walks and do water aerobics and
keep up your other activities and eat healthier. You may
be retired from work, but not from life, enjoy your life.
Everything you do involves breathing! So do it right and
do more of it, take nice full breaths quit breathing
shallow. Most all sleeping problems are because most
people don't breath correctly or they take shallow breaths
or stop breathing all together at night.

➢ Loose weight
➢ Lower my blood pressure
➢ Lower my cholesterol
➢ Reduce stress
➢ Energy chi development
➢ Meditation
➢ Philosophy
➢ Stretching
➢ Nutrition

**Tai-Chi Exercises or other exercises is key, you can do
about anything walking, swimming, dancing, aerobics,
yoga, etc.**

Life's Wonders

LIFE'S WONDERS

SENIORS OHAHA

SENIORS OHAHA
Body, Mind & Spirit

The Senior Advantage *Seniors have a great advantage over the younger generation. They have lived long enough to have seen the simple truths of life and have an amazing accumulation of knowledge through their life's experiences. Let's go back into time, seniors can appreciate the fact that all through life we seem to be in a great hurry. From the time we were born till now! We are in such a hurry to grow up and be an adult that we failed to notice that we left the most valuable things behind.*

THE BREATH OF LIFE *At birth when the breath of life first entered your body you're given life. Your parents and everyone are excited to welcome you here. As we grow and become a youth our society failed to teach us the most important and valuable things during our lives, was how to BREATH correctly. Yes, the correct way to breath! You see we all think that it's pretty natural to do, because we've done it since birth. and have always felt that that's all there is to it. We have never been so wrong about something that is so important to your entire life and existence. Breathing controls everything without it you cease to exist. Everything in your body depends on it to function properly. Think about it ,no air, no oxygen, no life! When we breath we place oxygen into our bodies. This creates the blood flow to deliver the oxygen to our body tissues and in return the fibro vascular system of the blood pushing through-out our body tissue and feeds our body and pushes the waste into our blood veins and sends it out. At the same time the lungs open and our bodies electrical system starts firing pumping the heart and other organs which produce what our body needs to function.*

Life's Wonders

LIFE'S WONDERS

SENIORS OHAHA

*You ask what does that have to do with you and Seniors Ohaha? Simple the older we get the less we breath. We start to breath shallow and sometime we stop breathing all together. We fail to understand that breathing controls everything from life to emotion, stress to tension and so much more. With out these things or an incorrect amount of these things can make our lives and body functions misfire and create imbalances in our bodies and lives. This misfire creates fear, stress, and emotions that you react to and the body functions try to tell us but only after a malfunction takes place in your system. Things like a heart attack, high blood pressure, emotional imbalances and so much more. These things are just simply telling you that you have a misfire and you need to fix it. You must **Simply Breath** and breath correctly. Breathing controls our ability to relax and recharge. Breathing incorrectly we're killing ourselves and making our quality of life miserable. It's amazing that something so simple controls so much. More than that something so easy to do correctly can make such a dramatic change in the quality of our life.*

Simply Breath *correctly and your life will change dramatically. Your entire life changes with more flexibility, body functions, enjoyment, fun, attitude. We will sleep better and awaken feeling so much better more relaxed and recharged. This one simple thing will open up a new life's meaning for us and help us enjoy life. Get ready to laugh, giggle, and smile. It flows with smooth expression and <u>comfort of experience</u>. Everything from eating to digestion, regain the energy to enjoy life, family and friends.*

Life's Wonders

SENIORS OHAHA

SENIORS OHAHA

Many people say I have been on the earth long enough to have been around the block once or twice. " Well now it's time to use that knowledge and experience. Remember the phrase "Relaxation within the effort" the use of all the experiences & knowledge you have seen and achieved in your lifetime! Let's use it now and bring the value to life back. Share it with family and friends. Have some fun with it ! Making life easier, eliminate pains and stiffness with more flexibility, better health, help your digestive system, improve your range of motion and strengthen and your mental attitude. At the same time you are learning an Ancient Martial Art of Kung-Fu senior style called Tai-Chi. All of the exercise motions are Martial Arts Kung-Fu moves. We have an Ancient Art of Tai-Chi that is designed specifically for the older population that is wonderful.

Features:

Greater range of Motion, Strength, Flexibility, Mental Control and Awareness promotes healthier eating, and digestive process and body functions, with amazingly more agility. It's the art of the seniors, it flows with expression and the smooth comfort of experience applying the use of relaxation within their effort. Make your life fun and enjoyable share the secrets of the breath of life with your family and friends.

Longevity 寿

Life's Wonders

LIFE'S WONDERS

SENIORS OHAHA

Your confidence and mental control absolutely establishes amazing and rewarding renewal of your personal life's wonders.

Seniors Ohaha *is for all ages, all people, from all walks of life. It will build core strength and coordination while Improving your balance. Organs and body functions return new production, strength, confidence and agility it needs.*

This is an easy to understand and easy to use program. It opens up a happier life for each person breathing and exercising with the Seniors Ohaha making daily life fun again and something to look forward to. The step by step instruction will guide each person to a level of confidence, flexibility, and a successful healthier life that you thought was gone forever.

Exercise is light and low impact filled with fun. This is something you can share with your friends and family that will bring everyone together in fun and enjoyment for many years to come. Try the Seniors Ohaha program and feel it's wonderful benefits.

*Remember you can use the Seniors Ohaha principals with other low impact exercises. Things like dancing, water aerobics, going for a walk and so many other thing you do daily just remember to **Simply Breath**. It's a way of life.*

Life's Wonders

SENIORS OHAHA

SENIORS OHAHA
Body, Mind & Spirit

THE ART OF BREATHING

We need to understand the concepts of breathing, it gives our body the oxygen and blood circulation and feeds the entire system. Learning to breath makes the circulator, respiratory and electrical system in compliment with the rheumatics of life's rhythm.

It makes it possible for us to have a collaboration of the body function that support from injuries and promotes healthier life and body functions. It is absolutely amazing how most people don't breath correctly. Some adults stop breathing in their sleep because they don't know how to relax and let their body recharge. They don't program their body to continue it 's functions. They breath improperly during the day and totally stop breathing at night. This is not only dangerous and threatens life, but is commonly known as sleep apnea. Seniors develop bad habits and bad health habits both at night and during the day.

To understand and get our bodies the oxygen it needs to grow breathing correctly is the first and basic power that we must conquer and achieve. Understanding the body delivers to all our muscles and organs the food of life, and strengthens us through this simple but most often denied function of oxygen. We will be up lifted with energy once we see and feel the difference. We will see and feel an immediate change. Start feeling a little light headed and or we will feel a tingling in our skin and hair.

Life's Wonders

LIFE'S WONDERS

SENIORS OHAHA

Breathing brings oxygen throughout the entire Body & Mind. It travels through the entire body, Inhaling and exhaling pulling oxygen from the top of our body to the bottom. Remember we need to let our body and mind work together from within our relaxation within the effort. Healing powers take over from the touch. From the top of the head to the bottom of the feet. Relax feel the oxygen travel through your body from one point to the other. Travel with your circulation throughout your universe (your body) feel, see, and hear yourself and it's your internal self rhythms. To be in harmony with the comfort of your own arithmetic's is an amazing discovery and such a relaxing and beautiful thing to find.

MENTAL POWERS. Telepathically communicate speaking to and through the Mind & Body traveling through your bodies system directing a cleaner communication. Learning how to travel and flow with this process in a great way of recharging the body and its functions. **Seniors Ohaha** will teach you to do a motion of motions that has been taught for thousands of years in the ancient Chinese culture. It shows you how to heal yourself and keep injury and healing powers that are given to us at birth that you have never tapped into. It's time that we understand the magic, strength yet the simplicity of your own mind and body.

COMPLETION, FLOW and ATTITUDE It's actually funny how this works. It will actually become easy, fast and comfortable if you let yourself have fun and be a reborn baby. A child again and feeling better, naturally your attitude will change and we will see things from a more positive and opened minded view.

Life's Wonders

Life's Wonders

SENIORS OHAHA

Seniors Ohaha a wonderful safe, secure and affordable way to regain so many wonderful aspects of life senior style. The first steps to a new enriched life. Being a personal care giving to yourself.

Most people *do not know* how to breath properly. Seniors for the most part, as they get older tend to breathe short or at night even stop breathing. I am going to show you how to restart and reprogram yourself to solve this problem. It will be fun, enjoyable and you will laugh when you see how easy it is.

We simply put the Oxygen back into the blood and it will naturally clean the body, feeds the body, and stimulate the body to produce enzymes and amino acids as well as the electrical system to engage and start firing again. The heart and your entire system will start working again in a natural way that it was designed to do just by simply breathing. And we will have a wonderful time doing it. As you hear and see this you will laugh with confidence of how simply it all is.

1. **Through Controlled Motivation** and reprogramming of your conscious mind and sub conscious mind. We can make this automatic daily function for you.
2. **Ancient Chinese exercise** secrets of very low impact exercises will make you feel so much more alive and give you the energy and drive to really enjoy life senior style.
3. **Simply breathing** and restoring life it's truly amazing.

Why do we say with each and every breath we take as we chant? How often do you breath? All the time, therefore the Subconscious Mind programs you and your chants to consistently be active.

SENIORS OHAHA

Breathe, Breathe, Breathe

Range of Motion *you will feel so much better*

Better Rest, Recharging and Sleeping *through the night.*

Digestive *no blotted stuffed feeling, better digestive system*

Mental attitude, Energy levels, Memory

Surgery recovery for Cancer, Heart, other medical conditions.

Controlled Motivation *It's something that is in itself a wonder of the world. You will Master in minutes.*

Alzheimer's: *Although Alzheimer's disease has many types of dementia. Vascular dementia tends to be related to blood flow issues. This is a tremendous help breathing and putting oxygen into the blood system, more consistent blood flow, better electrical response and body participation. Your entire body become more alive and aware mentally and physically.*

Secrets: *It's all about simply knowing the secrets*

Arthritis: *when you see and fell the opportunity for you to control the pains and stiffness of Arthritis your days and nights become yours again. To be able to sleep with so much less pain and stiffness is simply a joy. But to awaken in the mornings and start your day with Seniors Ohaha opens a whole new time in life for you. You will be excited again to get up and feel confident about your day.*

Light touch exercise *easy, fun exercises / walking the swimming pool / Walking / Dancing /*

Very low impact exercise */ Tai—Chi Kung —Fu seniors style* **Caregiver** *This will allow senior care again for themselves.* **Independence and self Freedom**

Life's Wonders

LIFE'S WONDERS

SENIORS OHAHA

Breathing *Take a deep breath,*

Inhale through the nose, exhaling through the mouth.
Do Not Shallow breath. *If light headedness occurs, simply stop the exercise. This exercise also has the effect of really opening up people physically. This exercise uses the body, mind and spirit to greatest efficiency.*

CAUTION! Especially older people: Never do panting or shallow breathing except while seated. Hyperventilation may occur. hyperventilation can be a problem because, of possible brief blackout could occur.

Breathing and exercise *A 20% reduction in oxygen to the blood levels may be caused by the aging process and normal breathing habits. Poor breathing robs energy and negatively affects mental alertness. Unless breathing is exercised, aging affects the* **respiratory system as follows: Stiffness:** *The rib cage and surrounding muscles get stiff causing inhalation to become more difficult. Less elasticity and weak muscles leave stale air in the tissues of the lungs and prevents fresh oxygen from reaching the blood stream.*

Rapid, Shallow Breathing: *This type of breathing, often caused by poor posture and weak or stiff muscles, leads to poor oxygen supply, respiratory disease, sluggishness, or heart disease. Sit up straight. Exhale through the mouth. Inhale through the nose and, at the same time relax your body.*
As you breathe you need to start **RE-PROGRAMING** *yourself so from now on your body and mind will engage your sub-conscious mind to take over for you.*

Life's Wonders

SENIORS OHAHA

BREATHE AND EXTEND YOUR LIFE.

From this moment on every time we take a breath,
We want to simply tell ourselves a short phase over and
over again. No matter what we do, we need to remind
ourselves to do the following with <u>each and every breath
we ever take</u> from now on. You're simply reprogramming
your body and mind, this is called <u>Controlled Motivation.</u>

From now on your body and mind are going to be put on
autopilot. You want your body and mind to naturally
respond every time you take a breath. We want to
program ourselves to be thinking and doing certain
things every moment that you take a breath. Feel yourself
breathe sit or stand up more erect, or if you start to read
or think the words **"breathe"** you automatically sit or
stand straighter and stretch your spine upward and smile
you will automatically feel better.

#1. Remind yourself to **relax** while breathing. Relax
actually let yourself-flow through your body (travel)
within the mind and help the body feel the relaxation
increasing.

#2. **Simply Breathe**! With a mental smile in yourself feel
the air flow into the nose and exhale through the mouth,
filling the lungs from the bottom of the abdomen you will
feel your lower back lift along with your chest and
shoulders. Relax... .

#3. In the next couple pages we will learn 4 phases that
you will teach your subconscious mind to say over and
over again
<u>**with each and every breath you take**</u>... .

Life's Wonders

SENIORS OHAHA

*Our **patience, understanding,** and **willingness** to deal with life and it's wonderful paths become easier and easier to deal with. We will learn to have total relaxation within the effort and it spreads to everything you do. You will find yourself being calmer and more patient. Now relax and let that inquisitive nature come to surface. The one that over the years has been held down for what ever reason. Let it grow again, learn to open up to yourself. It's ourselves that we need to learn from. We need to trust in ourselves and that is the power to reach within and relax and grow again. Quit holding yourself back, its ok to laugh, giggle feel free and relaxed. You see it's you that is making the pain and stiffness happen. Your body simply is doing what you are telling it to do or not to do.*

Communication *We need to call it up again, listen, hear, feel see and believe in ourselves again. Learn how to communicate again with ourselves tell your body to smile. Quit letting your body talk you into doing nothing as an answer. Talk back and reprogram your conscious mind, tell it that you wish to take the time and do this and to give you the support and energy to get it done. Explain to the conscious mind and the sub conscious mind that you need them to work in harmony to build and rebuild your healing process. To give you on command the extra energy to complete this program on a daily basis. You need to have a good working relationship with them, and direct the body to enjoy your continued growth. You may be in retirement but that doesn't mean your body is retired. You may be retired from work but not from life! Take control of your life and enjoy your Golden years. **They truly can be Golden!***

Life's Wonders

SENIORS OHAHA

Circulatory, Respiratory, Electrical System and Motion.
The sequence and uniformity with collaboration

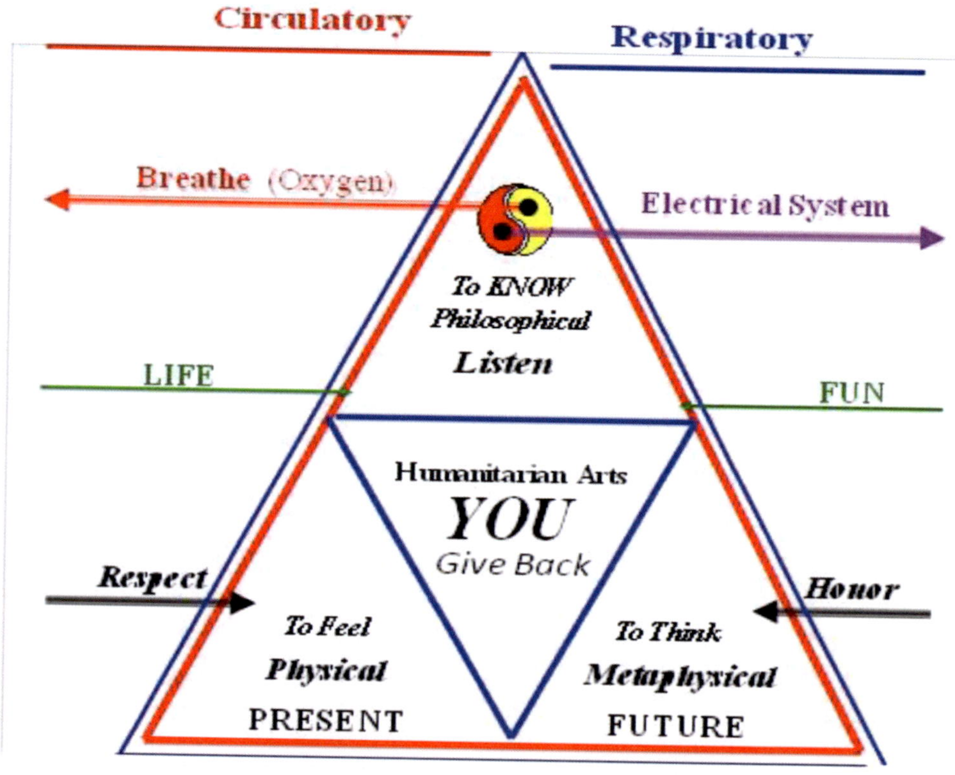

Circulatory   **Respiratory**

Breathe (Oxygen)   Electrical System

To KNOW
Philosophical
Listen

LIFE   FUN

Humanitarian Arts
YOU
Give Back

Respect   *Honor*

To Feel
Physical
PRESENT

To Think
Metaphysical
FUTURE

Now, the Magic, the hidden controls
are about to reveal the keys of life.

Life's Wonders

SEROR OHAHA

SENIORS OHAHA
Body, Mind & Spirit

Seniors Ohaha Exercise You must **practic**

Every day to re-train your body and mind to learn, how to breath and totally be recharged and relaxed while building a happier life and one of more control. It's really easy to do if you set your goals to do this **every morning** when you wake up, and **every evening** to help you go to sleep. You will find you awaken more recharged, happier and sleep more comfortably.

You must practice Seniors Ohaha Mental and Physical Exercises every day low impact.

Seniors Ohaha Tai-Chi is an Ancient Martial Art form of Kung-Fu designed seniors style called Tai-Chi. Share your Senior Ohaha with your friends and laugh with them as you ask them to come and practice Kung-fu with you seniors style. I assure you they will laugh and you'll have more fun than you've had in a long time. You may find that your friends will enjoy learning about Seniors Ohaha as well. You will laugh and enjoy how fun life's simplest things really are "Wonders". One of the secrets of life is to laugh and have some fun. Get ready to laugh, giggle, and a smile, you have earned it. It flows with the expression and comfort of experience and confidence of time.

Life's Wonders

LIFE'S WONDERS

SENIORS OHAHA

BODY FUNCTIONS. *YOU must understand, conquer and achieve getting your body the oxygen it needs to grow repair and build this first basic power. Understanding that the body delivers to all the muscles and organs the food of life and strength through this simple but most often denied function , breathing! You will be up lifted immediately with energy once we feel the difference. These all work independently yet in beautiful compliment together, independently but united.*

MOTION OF MOTIONS: *A rhythmic flow of circular motions that will give you the flexibility and direction of understanding of your body and how it should flow with an energy pattern that will charge you up with the grins and giggles of your youth. You will have so much fun and enjoyment you will feel guilty about feeling so good and having so much fun. Start to notice that it's all a very natural motion that you are doing. There are no hard or stressful moves or motions. No over extending or demand on our muscle groups. No taking risks yourself. Simply circular motions that allow you to rejoin yourself in harmony with yourself and body functions. You will learn to have more natural strength and range of motion through these circular motions.*

Life's Wonders

SENIORS OHAHA

Motion of Motions: *A rhythmic flow of circular and continuous motions that will give you the flexibility and understanding of our body and how it should flow within an energy pattern. This is done by use of an Ancient Chinese Martial Art of living and breathing called TAI-CHI.*

Motion of motions, combine the internal and external with the understanding and use of your internal natural rheumatic flow coordinated with your life functions. (Simply said Breathing) Let's keep it very simple. If you tie the life force of breathing, healing and controlled motivation (control) to something that you do 24-7 and make it a very natural function. Meaning you don t even have to think about It and it, takes place each and every day of your life.

Psychologists *believe the human mind has two systems for decision — making **Reasoning** and **Intuition** one on the left side of the brain and the other, the right side.*

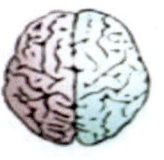

**Left Side of the Brain
REASONING Control**

**Right Side of the Brain
INTUTITION Emotion**

SIMPLY BREATHE *just by breathing correctly your life will change dramatically. your entire life changes with more flexibility, body functions, enjoyment, fun, attitude, you will sleep better and awaken feeling so much better more relaxed and recharged. The power of knowing and being more aware.*

Life's Wonders

LIFE'S WONDERS

SENIORS OHAHA

Sequence, Uniformity

The sequence, uniformity with collaboration of the respiratory, circulatory and electrical system promotes a healthier relationship between you and yourself. The inter-mind's eye if you may, a vision of communication that puts us into a meditative position with self. Simply said "Know Thy Self." you may never speak to others but you always speak to yourself. Now it's time to listen, hear, and see, what it is your body truly is saying. We need to listen how to fix it ourselves automatically through the natural ways that God provided us. If you will truly listen your body will guide you through this wonderful sophisticated system of ours, it really is pretty basic if we listen.

SEQUENCE AND UNIFORMITY / KUNG FU ANCIENT

ARTS. The marshal arts are a wonderful expression of self. Ancient movements that assist us throughout life and health cycle. Learning self-defense, moves and motions that are in complete harmony with in every motion. With each and every motion we will learn that we are actually using self- defense and Kung-fu moves that could make the difference in saving your life and or your loved ones. We must work at the pace that feels best. Reset your body alignment through breathing and soft motion. It's just nice to know we can take care of yourselves, and that all the things we learn have multiple uses and value.

Life's Wonders

LIFE'S WONDERS

SENIORS OHAHA

Seniors Ohaha Exercise: *The fun and amazing thing about Seniors Ohaha is that from the moment you awaken to the second that the you fall asleep, you will be enjoying what you have learned. Think of it like unplugging yourself at night and allow your body to recharge. The magic is constantly working for you 24-7 and that's wonderful.*

If you train yourself to do your breathing and soft touch massage before going to sleep every night you will put yourself into what I refer to as auto pilot. You will tell your body to continue breathing as trained all through the night. Tell your body to recharge and heal itself of it's injuries, aches and pains every night while you sleep.

You see your body and mind is your personal computer it will reboot and take care of you while you are sleeping and it actually works better and faster when you're relaxed and recharging. Simply train your conscious and sub conscious mind to work together automatically.

Breath through your nose, exhale through the mouth.

Morning Exercise: *Let's start with the second you awake in the morning before getting out of bed take 10 deep breaths, inhale through the nose and exhaling from your mouth. While you're still laying down do these breathing exercises, tell yourself to relax and take a deep breath, think and be really calm, breathe easy there is no hurry.*

Life's Wonders

SENIORS OHAHA

Morning Exercise continued:

Whatever you do don't make it a chore, relax and enjoy the comfort. Breath slow and relaxed. While taking these 10 deep breaths take your arms and cross them lightly across your chest and take your hands and touch softly from your elbows to your finger tips as you pull your hand across the arms, giving yourself a soft slow touch massage.

This will start your stimulation of the tissue. Now as you get to the hands rotate each hand so you give each hand a soft touch message and when you get to the fingers simply shake your fingers one at a time with your hand that just did the massage. Do it again with the other arm and hand. Now place your hand on top of the big part of your thumb mussel that holds the thumb and softly message the big thumb mussel and the skin between your thumb and index finger. Squeeze it softly not hard and not to vagarious.

Next this is very important, if you fall asleep don't worry you are finally just relaxing and it's good for you. When you awaken start again! You're in no hurry enjoy…

Now take 10 more breaths, through your nose and exhale from your mouth and at the same time bend your knees and slide your feet back and forth on the mattress. You are simply giving yourself a foot message, what's taking place is you're training your body to awaken totally recharged and relaxed. You're building with a wonderful communication line within your body.

Life's Wonders

LIFE'S WONDERS

SENIORS OHAHA

Seniors Ohaha Mornings * When you awaken *
Very Important before you get out of bed.

We are re-training and reprogramming your body to awaken without stiffness and stress and your mind to work naturally. Now take another 10 breaths in through the nose and exhale out the mouth, while you're doing this take your hands again and softly rub them lightly across your forehead and down to your chin, do this as you do the 10 breaths.

❖ **Take 7 breaths**
Through your nose and exhale out your mouth.
On the 7ᵗʰ breath roll to the side of your body that you normally sit up on to get out of bed
As you do this, sit up on the edge of the bed with your feet hanging down.

❖ Let's breath **another 7 times** through your nose and out your mouth, This time as you breath in pull your hands into your body and slide your hands up to your chest, while stretching your body, as the lungs fill with air. sit up straight

❖ As you exhale drop your hands back down to you lap do this **As you take 7 breaths.** On the seventh breath step off the bed and stand up next to the bed and walk away from the bed. As you are walking away notice that you are not feeling any pain or stiffness, notice that you're standing taller and felling pretty good. Can you imagine how you will feel if you do this every day. It's very important to re-train yourself how to awaken in the mornings, every morning you must train yourself to do this!

Life's Wonders

SENIORS OHAHA

BREATHING BEFORE GOING TO SLEEP.

Before going to sleep you want to do the same exercise as you did before getting up in the morning. If you do this you will sleep better and more relaxed. Breathing exercises when you are going to sleep has a couple additional things that will help you, it will release tension and stiffness help relieve pain from arthritis and generally let you relax for a good nights sleep. **Understand you are simply unplugging yourself from the daily stress and many things you pack around in your head all day long.**

Step 1.

Breath through your nose *and* **exhale through your mouth**. *While you inhale let the air in slowly stretch your back and feel your chest rise while laying down. Your back will release.*

Step 2. *Really relax breath deep and physically relax, Do this several times. As you breathe physically feel yourself relax more and more.* **While saying your chants and phrases that you learned earlier say to yourself each and every time you take a breath.**

1. **With each and every breath I take , I feel so relaxed, so much more relaxed than I have ever felt before.**

2. **With each and every breath I take , I feel so good, so much better than I have ever felt before.**

3. **With each and every breath I take, I feel so recharged, so much more recharged than I have ever felt before.**

Life's Wonders

Heart Attack & Water

You need your minimum water to help flush The toxins out of your body!

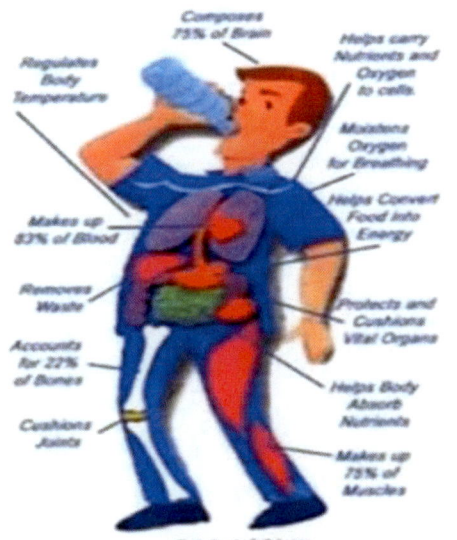

Correct time to drink water... Very Important. From A Cardiac specialist! *1 glass water at bed time Removes* toxins out of your body!

Drinking water at a certain time maximizes its effectiveness on the body:

2 glasses of water after waking up - helps activate internal organs 1 glass of water 30 minutes before a meal - helps digestion 1 glass of water before taking a bath - helps lower blood pressure 1 glass of water before going to bed - avoids stroke or heart attack

A doctor was asked why do we and other people urinate so much at night time. Answer from this cardiac doctor was gravity holds water in the lower part of your body when you are upright. When you lie down and the lower body (legs and other things) seeks level with the kidneys it is then that the kidneys remove the water because it is easier.

Life's Wonders

Bananas and your Health

So, a banana really is a natural remedy for many ills. When you compare it to an apple, it has four times the protein, twice the carbohydrate, three times the phosphorus, five times the vitamin A and iron, and twice the other vitamins and minerals. It is also rich in potassium and is one of the best value foods around. So maybe it's time to change that well-known phrase so that we say, 'A banana a day keeps the doctor away!'

Seniors Ohaha

Life's Wonders

Each and every year we face the Road of Life!

If we take the same road year after year we will always end up in the same place. In January of each year we look down that road. We always make New Year's resolutions, things like to lose weight, make more money, exercise or to make some kind of changes in life.

We go down that road year after year from January to December. Hoping to find the Path or turn that leads us to our secrets. The Secret path that leads us to Happiness, Success, Love, Joy, Knowledge, Riches, and Peace.

As we return Year after Year, We notice that There were many turns and paths along the way. Paths that you wished you would of, could of, and even should have gone down, but we passed up that opportunity, that chance of successes and winning.

We now understand we can control our direction. It's our road and our choices the directions we take. Our success is a right of our participation, and not just chance. Don't take the chance that you would walk by and miss any of your wonderful   opportunities in life.

Plan your road, know your direction, take a helicopter view of your Road of life. Look down and see where it goes and where the turns are now you see, where you should of, could of, or will turn this time. Make it Happen take Control of Your life.

It's all about You!

Which
Road
do I Take?

Life's Wonders

LIFE'S WONDERS

Road of Life

Each and every year we face the Road of Life. If we take the same road year after year we will always end up in the same place. In January of each year we look down that road. We always make New Years resolutions, like to loose weight, make more money, exercise or to make some kind of changes. We go down that Road Year after Year from January to December hoping to find the Path or turn that leads us to our Secrets of Life hoping to find the path that leads us to Happiness, success, Love, Joy, Hoping for Knowledge, Riches, and Peace. As we return Year after Year, We notice
that there were many turns and paths along the way. paths that you wished you would of, could of, and even should have gone down, but we passed up that opportunity or chance to successes and winning. We now understand we can control that Direction. It's our road and our choices and our directions we take. Our success is a right of our participation, and not just chance.   Don't take the chance that you would walk by or miss any   of the wonderful Opportunities in life. Plan your road,   know your direction, take a helicopter view of your road of life.   Look down and see where it goes and now you see, where you should of, could of, or even will turn this time. Make it Happen take Control of Your life.

It's all about You!

59

SENIORS OHAHA

SENIORS OHAHA

Seniors Ohaha PTSD

is an Ancient Chinese Art of Breathing and Living combined with the Chinese Art of Tai Chi Kung- Fu exercise giving you mental and physical control of controlled motivation thereby controlling Post Traumatic Stress Disorder and giving you back a greater quality of Life

"Breathe of Life"

Post Traumatic Stress Disorder

Hand in Hand my brothers and sisters, we will fight this battle together, and win...
SENIORS OHAHA and YOU!

LIFE'S WONDERS

The Author and Seniors Ohaha

Seniors Ohaha was designed and written by Professor Michael S. Sandos a Master in the Chinese Tai Chi Kung-Fu and Gung-Fu Mixed Martial Arts. Kajukenbo, Wun Hop Kuen Do and KOA Kajukenbo Ohana Association.

Master Sandos resides in Salt Lake City, Utah with his family. His passion for the arts and strong life skills promoted the writing of Seniors Ohaha. He has worked with thousands of people all over the world with years in the teaching and experiences of Mixed Martial Arts.

Senior Grand Master Sandos always loved teaching his students how to heal, not just hurt and protect. Using the Ancient Chinese Secret Art of Tai Chi, Michael observed older generations and rehab patients recover quicker, get stronger with more flexibility and range of motion, have better digestion, sleep better and awaken more alive and recharged. This is a study of motion of motions. Using the brain not just the brawn . A soft easy continuous motion of low impact exercise which gives the patient wonderful control. Through controlled motivation, breathing and exercise, people understand the body's need to have good strong oxygen in the blood to rebuild all body functions. He will help to teach you how to reprogram yourself so it's a automatic 24-7.

Senior Grand Master Sandos has been in the Martial Arts over 63 years representing the United States in 16 countries. Senior Grand Master Sandos taught as a veteran in the United States Navy many years during the Vietnam conflict. He currently is the Founding Director of the KOA council of Grand Masters Worldwide. When it comes to mental, physical, and philosophical training there's none better than Senior Grand Master Sandos. He specializes in the study of the brain. Conscious and Subconscious, Mind over Matter, the left and right side of the Brain. The understanding the And use of the Brain Waves, and Brain vibrations.

SENIORS OHAHA

SENIORS OHAHA

Recognizing
A Stroke

Awareness Helps!

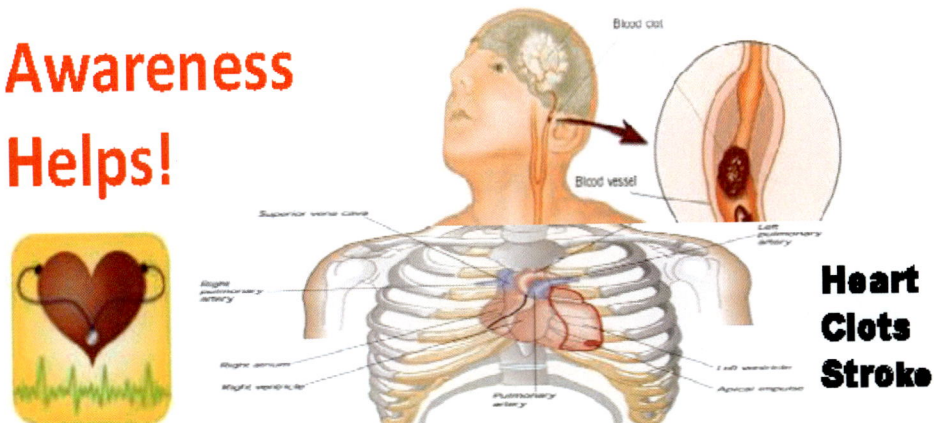

Heart
Clots
Stroke

Ask 3 Questions
Remember First 3 Letters **S T R**

S ~ Ask them to Smile?

T ~ Talk or Speak to You?

R ~ Raise Both ARMS

A New Sign of a Stroke

Ask them to stick out their tongue? If It's **'Crooked'** or goes to One Side or the Other, it's a sign of a Stroke.

Call 911   Life's Wonders

Lemons
& Health

Lemon (Citrus) is a miraculous product to **KILL CANCER CELLS**.
IT IS 10,000 TIMES STRONGER THAN CHEMOTHERAPY.
Why do we not know about that????
Because there are laboratories interested in making a synthetic version that will bring them HUGE PROFITS. You can now help a friend in need by letting them know that lemon juice is beneficial in PREVENTING the disease. Its taste is pleasant and it does NOT produce the horrific effects of chemotherapy.
If you can, plant a lemon tree in your garden or patio. How many people have to die, while this is a closely guarded secret , so as not to jeopardize the beneficial multimillionaires' large corporations?
As you know, the lemon tree does not occupy much space and is known for its varieties of lemons and limes. You can eat the fruit in different ways. You can eat the pulp, juice press, prepare drinks, sorbets, pastries,...the lemon is credited with many virtues, but the most interesting is the effect it produces on cysts and tumors!!! This plant is a proven remedy against ALL TYPES OF CANCER!!!! Some say it is very useful in all variants of cancer. It is considered also as an antimicrobial spectrum against BACTERIAL INFECTIONS AND FUNGI. EFFECTIVE AGAINST PARASITES AND WORMS. IT REGULATES BLOOD PRESSURE THAT IS TOO HIGH, IT IS AN ANTIDEPRESSANT, COMBATS STRESS AND NERVOUS DISORDERS!!!
The source of this information is fascinating. It comes from one of the largest manufacturers in the world, saying that more than 20 laboratory tests since 1970, the extracts revealed that it destroys the malignant cells in 12 TYPES OF CANCER, including colon, breast, prostate, lung and pancreas...
The compounds of this tree actually showed 10,000 times better than the product Adriamycin, a drug normally used chemotherapeutically in the world, by slowing the growth of cancer cells. And what is even more astonishing is this type of therapy with lemon extract not only destroys malignant cancer cells but does NOT affect healthy cells!!! Institute of Health Sciences, 819 N. L.L.C. Cause Street, Baltimore, MD 01201

HEALING BURNS

Healing burns Miracle for all burns
This is taught to beginner fireman.

1. Quickly First aid consists to spraying or **run cold water** on the affected Area. In spite of the pain until the heat is reduced and stops burning the layers of skin.

2. Then, spread egg whites on the affected are, after running cold water on the affected area (separated 2 egg white from the yolks, beat them slightly and dip hands or affected areas in the solution.) The whites then dried and formed a protective layer.

Egg white is a natural collagen and continued during at least one hour to apply layer upon layer of beaten egg white on affected areas. Within a couple hours no longer felt any pain and the next day there will hardly be a trace of the burn. 10 days later, very little to no trace will be left at all and skin will regained its normal color. The burned area totally regenerates thanks to the collagen in the egg whites, a placenta full of vitamins.

BURNS

LIFE'S WONDERS

SENIORS OHAHA

An Ancient Chinese Art of Breathing and Living combined with a Chinese art of Tai Chi Kung-Fu exercise. A journey of knowledge, experience and secrets of life for the young of all ages be a Seniors Ohaha black belt and join the battle Against Cancer, Heart Disease, PTSD for our vet's and all medical recovery patients

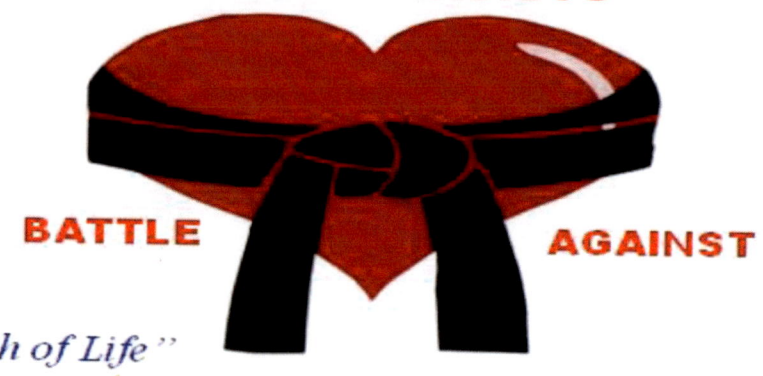

MARTIAL ARTISTS

BATTLE   AGAINST

"Breath of Life"

CANCER, HEART, PTSD

Seniors Ohaha is specifically designed for Seniors, Cancer, Heart and or all medical recovery patience. We have a wonderful responsibility to help, teach, understand and provide a second chance for folks when they have had either life or time taken away from them. They need to recover and take back the controls of life that is so deeply needed.

Seniors Ohaha allows you the pride to do and believe in something you can do and control for yourself. Something so fulfilling and rewarding of self motivation and regain control of your life and direction. To have something fun and physically enjoyable that you control. The frustration of loss of control is devastating, recover with Seniors Ohaha

Mind over Matter
Mind, Body, and Spirit

Life's Wonders
Seniors Ohaha
Success is yours
As a right of your
Participation

Congratulations
Today is the
Begging of the
Rest of your life

OPEN the Door to the Rest of your Life

Read this book 3 times then Start your Breathing Techniques, be sure to add your personal chants.

As you get more comfortable with this you will add **5 more chants** or phrases

As an example:

A. With each and every breath I take, I feel **Relaxed,** so much more **Relaxed** than I have ever felt before.

Thank you!
Professor Mike Sandos
Author Seniors Ohaha

Life's Wonders

LIFE'S WONDERS

Life's Wonders

Why do we say with each and every breath we take as we chant?
How often do you breath? All the time, therefore the Subconscious
Mind programs you and your chants to consistently be active.

Index
Introduction 1-4
Breathing 5, 6, 7, 8, 9, 10, 11, 12,
Brain Power the Third Eye 13, 14, 15, 16, 17, 18,
Mind over Matter 19, 20, 21, 22,
RAS Reticular Activating System 23, 24, 25,
Mind Control 26, 27, 28, 29,
Einstein Time and Space 30, 31,
Brain Waves 32, 33, 34, 35, 36, 37, 38,
Life Styles 39, 40, 41,
Life Styles Heart, Lungs, Brain, Oxygen 42, 43, 44, 45, 46, 47,
Seniors Ohaha 48, 49,
Tai Chi Science Brain Power 50, 51, 52, 53, 54,
Purpose 55, 56, 57, 58, 59, 60, 61, 62, 63
Function and use of Tools 64, 65, 66, 67
Controlled Motivation 68, 69, 70, 71, 72, 73, 74, 75, 76, 77, 78, 79, 80,
81, 82, 83, 84
Hidden Magic controls 85, 86, 87, 88, 89,
Exercises 90, 91, 92, 93,
Extra Health Tips 94, 95, 96, 97, 98, 99, 100- 101, 102, 103, 104, 105
106, 107,